Unix Handbook for Oracle DBA

Flavia D'Souza

www.Amazon.com

Unix Handbook for Oracle DBA

By **Flavia D'Souza**

Printing History

December   2010:   First Edition

ISBN-13: 978-1456355692

ISBN-10: 1456355694

This book is dedicated to the people who Inspire me to do what I enjoy to do and also to all DBA's who are responsible for some of the most challenging task in the world of Computing. I believe this book will help you and also inspire you to be a professional on the job.

Contents at a Glance

Contents

Chapter 16: Memory Usage and Monitoring

Chapter 17: Load Monitoring on Unix Server

Introduction

The "Unix Handbook for Oracle DBA" is a practical guide for Oracle DBA's working on Unix. It's from my collection for over 15 years of practical usage of these tips and techniques as a DBA on Unix Servers.

Intended Audience

This book is designed specially for DBA's and Database specialist who are working on unix servers

Here is the Chapter-by-Chapter Summary

All commands and tips in this book have syntax with description and explanation on output result. It has brief scripts which are useful on the job as an oracle DBA on Unix.

This book is organized into following topics.

Unix Operating System

What is an operating system, Unix as an Operating system, Main components of Unix operating system, Unix Kernel, Unix as an Multitask operating system, Unix Shell, Unix File system, Types of files in Unix operating system

Know inside Unix Operating System

What is Unix File system, Standard Unix File system Structure, What is a command, What is command option, Unix files, How to copy, rename or move files

How to play around Unix Operating System

File name substitution, Content search of file using grep, How do you display End of File, File monitoring using tail, Comparing file content, Standard Input, What is UNIX I/O redirection, Pipe command, tee command, Back ground command, Cut Command, Unix Commands, How to continue command on the next line

Files and File System on Unix

All you need to know about Files and File system on Unix, What is a file in Unix, What is a directory in Unix, What is HOME directory on Unix, How to navigate to other sub directories, Access permission on files and directories.

Permission and security with Files and Directories

Unix system security, Why Security?, File Permission, umask, set new value for umask

Managing Jobs and processes

What is a process, How to list processes, Display Unix Processes, What is a foreground process, What is a background process, Process Id on Unix system, Process Job number on Unix, Advantage of submitting jobs in background mode, How to switch process between background and foreground, How to list all active background processes, Control Key signals in Unix, How to kill process

Unix Shell

What is Unix Shell, Type of shells, Bourne shell (sh), Korn shell (ksh), Bash shell, C shell, Your working environment in Unix, Your unix environment file

Unix Environment and Command line

What is a command, Command name options argument(s), Why options?, What is command arguments?, Command Alias, How to create command alias, Shell Variables, On C Shell family, On Korn Shell family, Environment variable, Prompting Variables,

Secondary Prompt, File search path, Directory Search Path, Unix Environment File

Unix Shell and Programming

What is Unix Command line?, BASH and Korn Shell, How to create commands and programs, Shell script, Variables as place holders, How to assign values to variables, How to display the values of variables, For Loop, while and until statements, The case statements, if statement, Exit command and status, Combinations of Exit Statuses, The && Operator, The || operator, Operators used in shell, Arithmetic Operators, Break and continue statements, break, continue statement, Special variable, Positional Parameters, Arithmetic Operators, Read data from terminal

File Manipulation on Unix

grep command, Sort command, Specific field Sort, Numeric sort, Sort hints, Reverse Sort, Cut Command, awk utility, File processing using AWK, File usage (fuser), XARGS Utility - Construct argument lists and invoke utility, Locate files that contain certain strings

All about Text editing in Unix

vi editor, vi modes, vi commands in command mode, Yanking and cutting, Yanking and Pasting, un-delete command, Handy commands while using vi editor, Sed editor, Substitute command

Transfer files and directories between unix system

Introduction, ftp program, Open remote host connection, scp for secured file copy, ssh program, How to setup passphrase authentication

Unix File System and Disk Management

Logical Volume Management (LVM), What is Logical Volume Management..?, List logical Volumes in HP-UX, Display Unix Mount Points, Display Mount Points in HP-UX, Display mount points in AIX and Solaris, Show Mount Points for a Physical Disk in AIX

Backup and Restore File System

Backup using CPIO, Backup ORACLE_HOME using CPIO, Verify backup using CPIO, Verify backed up files match with the original directory structure, Restoring files with CPIO, Backup using tar, Compress files, Backup using dump, Restoring files with dump

Unix System Parameters

Display Server Device Values, Display System Kernel Parameters, HP Tru64 Unix-Based Systems, HP-UX Based Systems, AIX Based Systems, Linux based Systems,Unix system Information, Random Access Memory, Swap Space, Some of the handy commands, nslookup (Query Internet domain name servers), netstat, MKNOD Special file, The Syntax to use named pipe with oracle export, The Syntax to use named pipe with oracle import, Cron, Crontab options, Database TIMEZONE, Time Zone Parameters for Databases, 16. Check the Database Character Set, Operating system info on Unix, To print name of current system, Semaphore Management, Display Values for Semaphores, Count used Semaphores, Determine the Semaphore sets held by an Instance, How to check semaphores on unix server?, Semaphore Parameters, Change Kernel Parameters

Memory Usage and Monitoring

Display RAM Size on Unix, Display RAM Size in Solaris, Display RAM Size in AIX, Display RAM Size in HP-UX, Display RAM Size in DEC Unix, Use svmon in AIX, Display allocated Memory Segments, Determining which instance owns which shared memory & semaphore segments, Running "oradebug" in Orcale 8, Running "oradebug" in Oracle9i, Manually De allocate a Memory Segment, Displaying the number of CPU processors in UNIX, Commands to display number of CPU, Display the number of CPUs on AIX, Display the number of CPUs in Solaris, System Configuration and diagnostic information.

Load Monitoring on Unix Server

Performance Monitoring, CPU usage and Processes, Using top, Using sar, CPU report using sar command, Swapping and memory switching activity using sar, Buffer activity report using sar command, prstat, vmstat, Show Server Load Average, iostat, CPU Utilization Report, Device Utilization Report.

Useful scripts for Oracle DBA

Temporary tablespace usage monitoring, Unix wrapper to check Single database, Unix wrapper to check Multiple database, Actual Database size used, Allocated space to database, Open Cursors, Currently opened cursors, Cursors open by username & Machine, Find SQL statement associated with cached cursors, Datafile Corruption investigation, Find table High water mark, Capture SID and serial# for a given database user to kill sessions, Backup ORACLE_HOME using CPIO, Restoring files with CPIO, Backup using tar, Statspack Collection Level, Set tracing on/off, Autorace utility for SQL Tuning, Explain plan fo SQL tuning, Softlink creation, dot profile (.profile), Useful unix Scripts constructs, Find documented init.ora parameters, Find undocumented init.ora parameters, List rman backups into spool file.

Writing this book was quite challenging, interesting and also satisfying, given that I have a reference book which addresses most of the challenges related to the Title faced by DBA's on the job working on Unix Server which I believe would be very useful to intended Audience.

Few years ago when I was looking for something similar, I could not find one, and I have not found even at the time of writing this book which could quite parallel the tips and techniques covered in this book which are practical, handy and easy to understand and apply.

Part 1

Chapter 1
Unix operating System

What is an operating system

Any computer has two major components hardware and software. If you have to successfully run any software on the hardware, you need a system that once again comprises of bunch of programs. This system acts as a coordinator between hardware and software. The most important part of an operating system in any computer is, it is the component that allows you to make use of the facilities provided by the system.

Unix as an Operating system

Unix operating system has a long history dated back to 1960's . It has undergone quite a lot of changes since it's first version way back in 1969. First version of unix was created by two system engineers at AT&T's Bell Labs named Kenneth Thompson and Dennis Ritchie. However commercial version was first made available by Interactive Systems Corporation after many modification in 1977.

Unix operating system which was first developed in late 1960s, has been under constant development ever since. Basically Unix operating system is suite of programs, which make the computer work. It is multi-user, multi-tasking system for servers, desktops and laptops.

These days we have many versions, flavours of Unix operating system by different vendors such as Solaris, AIX, Linux, HP/Unix etc

In spite of numerous number of flavours of Unix operating system they basically fall into 2 main categories/versions System V and BSD

What are the main components of Unix operating system

Unix operating system comprises of main 3 components

1. Unix Kernel
2. Unix Shell
3. Unix File system

What is Unix Kernel

The word kernel refers to the central component in any operating system. In unix kernel is indeed the central component which is responsible for managing the entire resources of the unix operating system.

Kernel has some important functions such as

- Manage Computer memory and allocate memory to processes based on priority
- Handle Instructions from shell and handle interrupts
- Most importantly schedule the work carried out by CPU
- Maintain file system by enforcing the permission

In any operating system usually file containing the Kernel is located in root directory and name of the kernel file usually include the letters **nix**

Unix kernel comprises of bunch of programs, and each program has it's unique function. Among many such programs Unix scheduler plays a critical role with respect to resource management

Unix as an Multitask operating system

Unix system allows multiple users to login at any given point in time and share resources by respecting all users with appropriate priority. This multi user resource sharing is handled by a program called unix scheduler in unix operating system. This resource sharing is also called time sharing.

Whenever a user runs a program, the program code is copied from disk to memory. Any program code loaded into memory and doing something is called process. Based on the task and the length of the program code, any process would spend few seconds to few minutes in memory. If you have multiple users running process at the same time, with relatively intensive task, you probably notice that there is no sufficient memory left to service this request. As a result processing would slow down and this is normally referred as memory shortage in the computer.

In olden days we used to have only one CPU (Central processing Unit) in any given computer that is suppose to handle all the task. These days we have larger capacity computers with multiple CPU's operating in parallel. Whether we use one CPU or multiple CPU's, you normally find number of processes outnumber the number of CPU's. So how is this multiple task handled by a given CPU at any given time?

Suppose you have 8 processes running at the same time and you have only one CPU in your computer. The unix scheduler allows the first process to run for some fraction of a second, then it suspends the first process and schedules the second for some fraction of seconds and then third and so on. The whole process repeats again until the entire process is completed. This time-sharing is done in a fraction of seconds and any user would not notice that his or her task is temporarily stopped for few short period of time. Nevertheless as the number of processes increase, overall throughput would be poor and eventually user does notice that a task, which had completed in the morning in 2 minutes has taken 8 minutes in the late afternoon. This is just because there were too may processes to service in the late afternoon and there were only few in the morning.

Unix scheduler can handle and track few hundred processes from several users at the same time. Any given user can run multiple programs at the same time. The unix schedule task is to manage all these processes and serve all the users simultaneously, though unix scheduler serves them at a time

Well it is fine with unix scheduler managing the multiple processes by suspending them temporarily in order to serve all processes equally. How about the memory in the computer system. What if we run out of memory and there is not sufficient memory to load several hundred programs into memory from disk.

As it is scheduled with the CPU, likewise the memory is also allocated to individual process. Whenever a process is suspended or temporarily stopped and if unix scheduler finds that there is a shortage of memory, the process gets copied to disk from memory. The new program gets loaded to memory and the process of copying programs back and forth from disk to memory and back to disk continues until scheduler finds sufficient memory to retail programs in the memory until they complete execution. This concept in computers is called swapping.

What is Unix Shell

Technically unix shell is a program. This program provides user interface when you login to unix system. This program is also called command interpreter because it interprets all the commands you enter at the unix prompt and passes it to unix operating system kernel for further action.

This shell is a program, which acts as a mediator between you as a user and the Kernel forming a shell. Whenever you login to unix system, you get your own copy of this shell program, so that you get to do things without interfering with other users. Each shell copy comes with it's own environment customised for individual user.

There are few shell's available today and they can be made available on any flavours of unix system. Though most of the syntax is common across all shells, there is variation.

Some of the Unix shells are Korn shell, Bourne shell, C shell , Bash shell etc

While working on unix system, you can easily switch between different shells and normally multiple shells would be available on any given unix operating system

What is Unix File system

After all we use computer system to process information. Having said that we need to store and organize this information in easily readable accessible format. In all computer system information is stored in the form of files and these files are organized in different folders called directories. On unix file system logical collection of files along with organized structure of directories collectively form File system.

Type of files in Unix operating system

Though files are entities that store the information, on unix operating system there are varieties of files

- Regular/Ordinary files
- Special files
- Pipes
- Socket
- Door
- Symbolic link
- Directories

Regular/Ordinary files :- These files normally contain test information or images, which can be edited . When you create ordinary files, you own the permission to control who has the permission to access. These ordinary files are organized within a directory. Actually files don't reside within directories, rather they hold the information to point to the actual location. A directory contains filename and inode number of the file.

Filename is used by the directory to locate the file and inode number acts as a pointer to find actual information about the file.

Special files :- On unix operating system physical devices such as terminal, printer, keyboard, tape drive are all treated as files. The advantage of treating these devices as files is, you can redirect output of a command to these devices as files, just like you redirect the output to ordinary files.

Note:- You notice in later part of this book when we redirect output from commands to a special device called /dev/null. On unix system /dev/null is treated as a special device file under /dev directory. On unix system /dev/null can be used to redirect unwanted output.

Pipes :- This is a link where unix connects two commands when they are communicating each other. This link acts as temporary file for the duration of inter process communication exists. This file hold data temporarily from one process until it is read by another. This file is called pipe. The purpose of the pipe file is to connect two unix processes and hold data temporarily. The standard output from one process is passed to another process as standard input and this is done using the pipe.

The pipe file is marked with **p** as the first letter of the permissions string

For example
prw-r----- /dev/xconsole

Socket :- This is yet another file type used for inter process communication. In this case, in addition to sending data, process can also send file descriptors to another process as standard input, using this socket file. File descriptor is an abstract key for accessing a file.

The socket file is marked with **s** as the first letter of the permissions string

For example

srwxrwxrwx X0

Door :- This yet another variety of special file inter-process communication between a client and server, currently implemented in Sun solaris unix operating system

The door file is marked with **D** (upper case) as the first letter of the permissions string.

For example

Dr--r--r-- name_service_door

Symbolic Link :- This is another file type on unix operating system, used to reference some other file. This symbolic link will have it's own name, but when you try to access this, or try to read or write, it basically reference these operations to file it points to.

The symbolic link file is marked with **l** as the first letter of the permissions string

For example
lrwxrwxrwx   init.ora -> /home/oracle/initsid.ora

Directories:- On unix systems directory is the most common file, They are like folders where you organize your files. Directories also contain files and other directories.

A directory is marked with **d** as the first letter of the permissions field.
e.g

drwxr-xr-x

Oracle Handbook for Oracle DBA

Chapter 2

Know inside Unix
Operating system

When you are ready to login to your unix system, system would great you with the prompt. Normally when unix system is started and ready to login it prints

login:

You enter your username followed by password should log you inside the unix system. Remember unix system is case sensitive.

Once you are successfully logged into the unix system you automatically land in your HOME directory. Unix system also display a prompt string. Usually it is "S". However the prompt string can be customized. More on this customization later.

$

Any UNIX system can have many users on it at any one time. Usually user's home directories are grouped together under a system directory such as /home.

Computer systems are popular for processing the information and unix system is no exception. As mentioned in the previous chapter information is stored in the files and files are logically organized in special files called directories.

What is Unix File system

File stores smallest information and related files are grouped under directories. It makes sense to logically group directories under certain entities called main directories and finally all main directories branch out from a root directory. This whole logical layout of the files and directories form Unix file system.

Entire Unix file system is logically organised as a hierarchy of directories. The starting directory in unix file system is called root directory and it is represented by a / (slash)

Standard Unix File system Structure

Usually you see a list of directories under root (/) directory. The details under each directory may vary from system to system

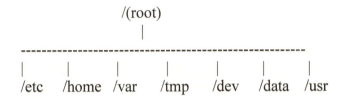

Note:- Kernal file is located in /(root) directory.

What is command

A command is something that tells unix operating system to do something.
Once you login to unix system, you get a prompt which is an indication that you are ready to type the command.

For example:-

If you type "who" at the command prompt, this would display information about all users currently logged into the system

$who

```
oracle    pts/2    Aug 26 11:51    (proddm)
oracle    pts/3    Aug 26 11:55    (proddm)
oracle    pts/4    Aug 25 07:25    (proddm)
```

oracle   pts/5   Aug 25 09:17   (proddm)

You always need to enter RETURN key which is Enter key on your keyboard that signals the operating system that you have finished typing the command

If you do a typing error while typing commands, unix system responds with message

$whos

whos: not found

Similarly "ls" is an another command that lists all files and directories under current directory.

$ls

What is command option

When you type in commands at the unix prompt, unix operating system displays information. It also has the provision to filter your displayed information or get more information by adding some flags. These additional, optional flags entered along with commands are called "command options"

In above example command "ls" would list files and directories under current directory.

$ls

create.sql
exp.log
exp.par
tmp

If you enter the command "ls –l" , this would list files and
directories with their permission and some other additional
information

$ls -l

-rw-rw-rw- 1 oracle   oinstall   885 Aug 26 05:00
exp.log
-rw-r--r-- 1 oracle   oinstall   2683 Aug 25 21:49 create.sql
-rw-r--r-- 1 oracle   oinstall   44829 Aug 26 13:05 exp.par
drwx------ 2 root   root   249 Aug 25 06:00 tmp

Unix system comes with huge bundle of commands, likewise
it also has various command options.

Once you login to unix system you would be identified by
your userid. To find out your own user id, you could use (id,
who am i) commands

id

uid=603(oracle) gid=606(oinstall)

who am I

oracle   pts/13   Aug 26 10:44   (proddm)

What is you want to switch to another user id say "oracle9i"
in unix system

Use "su" command to switch to another user id. "**su**" stands
for switch user

su oracle9i
password: enter password for oracle9i

pwd
/home/oracle9i
who am i

oracle9i   pts/13   Aug 26 14:32   (proddm)

To exit out of oracle9i account use **"exit"** command

Unix files

To create file you could use "cat" command

For example

Scat > myfile
John
Joseph
Serra
CTRL-d
$

Above example when you type "cat >filename" and enter, unix system would wait for you to enter the content of your file. Once you are done with typing the content of the file, enter "CTRL-d" to close the file.

The above process would create a file called **"myfile"** in your current working directory
You can also use cat command to display the content of the file "myfile"

cat myfile

The above command displays the content in one go.

What if your file is huge and cannot be displayed in one page, you could use "more" or "pg" command based on type of Unix system your are using to display the content of your file one page at a time

cat myfile|more
cat myfile|pg

When you use "cat myfile|more" command use space bar on your keyboard to go to next page.

When you use "cat myfile|pg" command use enter key on your keyboard to go to next page.

You also notice | in between two commands. This is called pipe and more on this in later chapters.

How to copy, rename or move files

Often when you work with script file on unix, you may want to save a copy of original file. To make a copy of the file use "cp" command

cp script.sql   script.sql_bak

Above command makes a copy of file "script.sql" and stores in "script.sql_bak"

Once you complete editing your script file and would like to give a meaningful name to your script file, you could use "mv" command to achieve this.

mv script.sql rman_bakup.sql

Above command renames file "script.sql" to "rman_bakup.sql"

Chapter 3

How to play around Unix Operating System

File name substitution

We use computers predominantly to process information. Information is stored and processed in files. Many times there would be a requirement to search, handle, process multiple files.

One of the powerful features of unix operating system is ability to handle file name substitution. File name substitution is done using "metacharacters".

There are mainly three file matching metacharacters in Unix operating system

1. Matching multiple characters using asterisk (*)

Suppose you have multiple files in current directory, some with extension "sql" and some with extension "sh" and some with "cmd"

What if you would like to list all files in your current working directory with extension "sql" only. The command below would list all files with extension "sql"

ls *.sql

Asterisk meta character can also be substituted for filenames.

For example you would like to list all files in your current working directory that starts with the letter "c"

ls c*

If you would like to list files having character "t" in the filename, you could use following command.

Chapter 3: How to play around Unix Operating System

ls *t*

Note:- asterisk (*) letter substitutes for any number of characters.

2. Matching single character using question mark (?)

What if you don't want to match multiple characters, rather match up only one character. The asterisk matches zero or more of any character, the question mark (?) matches *exactly one* character.

Suppose your current directory has files

chapter1, chapter2, chapter3, chapter4, chapter5, chapter10, chapter201, chapter100

If you type the command

ls chapter?

The above command will list all files except chapter10, chapter201, chapter100

You can use multiple (?) question marks to substitute for multiple characters.

For example if you want to list only the file chapter10, you could use the command

ls chapter??

This above command would list only the file chapter10

3. Use double brackets for variety for selection

What if you would like to list filenames with multiple permutation and combination, where each and every character position in the filename can be selected. This can be achieved by using double brackets

Suppose you have following files in your current working directory

chapter122, chapter222, chapter342, chapter412, chapter57, chapter10, chapter201, chapter100

If you issue a command in your current directory

ls chapter[1]*

The above command would list all files with string "chapter" and having digit "1" after this string followed by any matching character.

For example this would list files

chapter122, chapter10, chapter100

If you issue the command

ls chapter[12]*

This would list following files

chapter122, chapter222, chapter10, chapter201, chapter100

If you issue the command

ls *[2-9]

This would list following files

chapter122, chapter222, chapter342, chapter412, chapter57

Note: - Range of values within the brackets substitute for a particular character position in the filename

Content search of file using grep

In above examples we listed files using file substitution. What if you want to further narrow down your search to certain files that matches particular character patterns.

Unix system has a very handy command to list files, that matches certain pattern and it is called "grep"

The general syntax to use "grep" command is

grep pattern files

The pattern is normally a string of character. Every line of each file that contains pattern would be displayed at the terminal.

Each matching filename is displayed before the line matching the pattern, which helps to identify the filenames

For example

grep ora oracleinstall.log

The above command lists all lines in "oracleinstall.log" file matching pattern "ora"

Since unix system is case sensitive in nature, To address this issue in pattern use

grep [Oo]ra oracleinstall.log

The above command lists all lines in "oracleinstall.log" file matching pattern "ora"

or "Ora"

Like wise the following command lists all lines in all files under current directory that match pattern "ora" or "Ora"

grep [Oo]ra *

Some times when you have huge number files to search the patterns and also each file contains multiple occurrences of patterns, your output from command would be too large and also too confusing to scan the entire list.

What if you only interested in finding the filenames having the pattern

grep –l [Oo]ra *

The above command would list only filenames having the pattern "Ora" or "ora". Each matching filename is listed only once in the output.

To filter the pattern further, it can be enclosed within quotes

For example

grep "Amanda, cook" directory.lst

How about if you want to list files having special character such as *

Since * has special meaning to shell, you need to enclose this character with single quotes ' '

grep '*' directory.lst

How do you display End of File

Suppose you want to inspect a backup log file, to check the status of the backup and meantime do not want to scan the entire file, you could use "tail" command to check the end of file lines.

"tail" is a command or program on unix operating system used to display the last few lines of a test file.

tail oracleinstall.log

The above command displays the last 10 lines of "oracleinstall.log"

By default last 10 lines would be displayed, however you could control the number of lines displayed by using an option as follows

tail -100 oracleinstall.log

In above example last 100 lines of "oracleinstall.log" would be displayed

What if you want to display all lines except first 20 lines

tail –n +20 oracleinstall.log

Above command displays the entire file except the first 20 lines

File monitoring using tail

"tail" command has a special file monitoring option called follow (-f) which is very handy to observe the output of a backup log file or installation log file.

For example you have just kicked off an rman backup on one of the large database, and you would like to monitor the status of the backup as it gets backed up. You could use tail –f option to do this

tail –f rmanbackup.log

The above command helps you to monitor the rmanbackup.log as it gets written by rman while backup is still on.

Note:- To interrupt tail –f while it is monitoring, break-in with Ctrl+C

Comparing file content

Suppose you want to compare two similar files, to see what are the differences between the two files.

Unix system has a command called "diff" to find the difference between two files. The mismatching lines in each files would be displayed

For example

diff file1 file2

8a9

> line 10

The additional lines in file1 is prefixed by < and additional lines in file2 is prefixed by >

The above output indicated file2 has additional line with content "line10"

8a9 indicates the above line needs to be added between line number 8 and line number 9 in file1 to make both file1 and file2 identical

If you want to display the content of both files side by side you could use "sdiff" command

For example

sdiff file1 file2

Above command displays the content of file1 and file2 side by side on your terminal along with indicating differences.

If you are comparing 2 large files, it may not be practical to display the content of both files on your screen, Unix system has a option to suppress the identical lines and display only the differences. Use option "sdiff –s" for this

For example

sdiff -s readme.txt readme1.txt

8a9

> line 10

Note:- If you compare "**diff file1 file2**" and "**sdiff –s file1 file2**" command, the output is basically same. Use any command you like

If you want to ignore the case of letters and blank spaces, you could use another option with diff command. This option is – iw

diff –iw file1 file2

In above command Lines in the two files that differ only in case and by the number of spaces they contain are considered to be identical.

When you type a command in Unix system you get output if the command is run successfully. If not you normally see a message called "no found" when you type in the wrong command

For example

date

Friday, 28 August 2010 1:06:00 AM UTC

daat

ksh: daat: not found

In first scenario the output is called standard output and in second scenario it is called standard error. In this case both are written to the terminal.

In general when a command is carried out successfully, the result is sent to the standard output file. If the command fails to execute successfully the result is displayed on the standard error file (your terminal by default in both cases).

Standard output and stand error can also be redirected to a file using redirection (greater than) symbol >

Standard Input

Any command on unix system reads its input from standard input. By default this place happens to be your keyboard. And by default standard output and also standard error is written to terminal

To explain the concept of standard input type "cat" at your prompt. This command waits for user input. You can type any text you like and when you are done enter (CTRL-d) to end the file

$cat

John

Joseph

Stephan

CTRL-d

$

The test you entered in this case is treated as on standard input device. However CTRL-d is used to terminate the input.

Standard input can also come from a file or an output from another command instead of terminal. To redirect the content in the form of standard input (less than) symbol < is used

For example

$grep string < `cat filename`

What is UNIX I/O redirection

In unix system any standard input, standard output and standard error can be redirected to a place other than it's default device. This redirection is implemented by placing redirection characters between commands.

For example

date > std_output.log

The command "date" is executed and the output is written to file called "std_output.log". In this case you do not see any output from command "date" on your terminal. The output from date command is redirected to a file.

Note:- If file "std_output.log" contains any content it will be overwritten by the output of "date" command

You could append the output from "date" command to "std_output.log" by using the operator >>

date >> std_output.log

In following example standard input is redirected from a file called "**std_input**"

grep "george" < std_input

In above command the content of file "std_input" is fed to grep command. The standard input is redirected from a file.

standard input can also come from the output of another command

grep "george" < `cat users`

In this example "users" is a file and output from "cat users" command is redirected to grep as standard input.

Note:- commands within the commands are enclosed with operator (`)

However the output from the above command will be written to terminal. Once again this output can be redirected to a file using operator > as follows

grep "george" < `cat users` > std_output.log

The above command combines the two redirection capabilities.

In unix terminology Standard Input **(stdin),** Standard Output **(stdout),** and Standard Error **(stderr)** is called unix File descriptors. File descriptors can be represented by standard file handles and these handles are represented by unique numbers

Handle Number	Description
0	Standard input
1	Standard output
2	Standard error

For example:-

date 2> std_error.log

In above command all standard errors are redirected to **"std_error.log"** file

If you want to combine all three redirections in one command

grep "george" < `cat users` > std_output.log 2>&1

In above command standard input comes from output of command "cat users". Standard output is written to "std_output.log" file. Standard error represented by number "2" is redirected to standard output that is represented by number "1" in the background. Operator "&" represents background process

Pipe command

We know that from above examples, the output from one command can be used as standard input to another command. What if you want to further filter the output from first command and then feed this output as standard input to second command.

This can be done by using a connection link called **pipe** which allows you to connect two or more than two commands together.

Pipe enables you to take the output from one command and feed it directly into the input of another command

For example

ls –l |grep oracle

In above command "ls –l" command lists all files in current directory and pipes it to "grep oracle" command where it is further filtered to list the file names containing string oracle. As a default the output is written to standard output device that is terminal

tee command

What if you want to redirect the output from a command to a standard output file and at the same time you want to see the output on the screen. This can be done using tee command. "tee" command outputs the result in two direction. One copy to standard output file and one copy to terminal.

For example

ls –l |tee list_files.log

When you run above command "ls –l" command lists all files in current working directory and sends the list to standard output file **"list_files.log",** at the same time list of files would be displayed on the **terminal**

Back ground command

Normally when you run a command at the command prompt, your command prompt doesn't written until the command execution completes. what if you run a command that takes few minutes to complete or even longer. You probably don't want to wait for the command to return your command prompt to type in your next command.

Situations like this, you could make use of the facility in unix system called "running command in background mode". All you do is type in command followed by the ampersand character "&"

For example

rman_bkp.sh > rman_bkp.log &

The above command will be executed in the background. Meantime it will free up your terminal prompt and will be available for other task.

Whenever a job is assigned to run in background mode, unix system will assign an unique process id for the job, which will be displayed at your terminal, as soon as you submit your job. This process id can be used to monitor your job in general. More on this in later chapters

Cut Command

cut command cuts out (extracts) columns from a table or fields from each line in a file. Fields may be specified by numerical position or in terms of character offset. By default, fields are taken to be separated by white space. Another delimiter may be specified instead.

cut command cut's out selected fields of each line of a file. use the cut utility to cut out columns from a table or fields from each line of a file;

Options are interpreted as follows:

list

> A comma-separated list of integer *byte* (-b option), *character* (-c option), or *field* (-f option) numbers, in increasing order, with optional - to indicate ranges. For example:

> 1,4,7

> Positions 1, 4, and 7.

> 1-3,8

> Positions 1 through 3 and 8.

> -5,10

> Positions 1 through 5 and 10.

> 3-

> Position 3 through last position.

-b *list*

> Cut based on a list of bytes. Each selected byte is output unless the -n option is also specified.

-c *list*

> Cut based on character positions specified by *list* (-c 1-72 extracts the first 72 characters of each line).

-f *list*

Where *list* is a list of fields assumed to be separated in the file by a delimiter character (see -d); for example, -f 1,7 copies the first and seventh field only. Lines with no field delimiters will be passed through intact (useful for table subheadings), unless -s is specified.

-d *char*

The character following -d is the field delimiter (-f option only). Default is *tab*. Space or other characters with special meaning to the shell must be quoted. Adjacent field delimiters delimit null fields. *char* may be an international code set character.

-n

Do not split characters. If the high end of a range within a list is not the last byte of a character, that character is not included in the output. However, if the low end of a range within a list is not the first byte of a character, the entire character *is* included in the output."

-s

Suppresses lines with no delimiter characters when using -f option. Unless -s is specified, lines with no delimiters appear in the output without alteration.

Examples:-

Password file mapping of user ID to user names:

cut -d : -f 1,5 /etc/passwd

Unix Commands

Multiple commands on the same Line

Unix lets you to run a single command on a line and also run multiple commands on a line. When you run multiple independent commands on a line you need to separate them by semicolon **(;)**

There is no limit on number of commands you can string out on a given line, as long as they are separated by semicolon **(;)**

Output from each command is displayed on a new line as follows

For example

who am i; pwd;date

oracle   pts/13   Aug 26 10:44   (unpadm)

/home/oracle

Friday, 28 August 2009 3:23:52 PM EST

How to continue command on the next line

Well what if your single command itself spans more than a line ?. You could type your entire command in multiple lines by using \ (backslash).

You can insert a backslash character at the end of the line and continue the command on the following line.

**$echo my **

**userid **

37

is \

oracle

my userid is oracle

$

Part 2

Chapter 4

Files and File System on Unix

All you need to know about Files and File system on Unix

Computer systems are always busy processing the information. This information needs to be stored somewhere in the system. If we don't organize this information, it would be difficult to access, process and retrieve the valuable information in right time. To facilitate this massive information, unix systems have an information filing system in an organized way that is called file system.

In simple terms entire Unix file system is made up of files and directories

What is a file in Unix

Files are the smallest units where information is stored. File is a collection of data stored on disk. As we discussed in the previous chapters, information can be of different type and to accommodate different variety of information and functionality, we have classified the files as

- Regular/Ordinary files
- Special files
- Pipes
- Socket
- Door
- Symbolic link
- Directories

What is a directory in Unix

All the files in Unix are organized within directories and all directories are further organised based on the functionality in hierarchical fashion. On top of the list we have root directory represented by / (slash). Group of files forms a directory.

In entire Unix file system we have two types of directories

- Root directory
- Sub directory.

Root directory :- is on top of the unix file system and represented by / (slash) . This directory cannot be deleted or renamed and as the name indicates it is the root of unix file system

Sub directory :- Under root directory there are several subdirectories organized based on the type of files they hold. Unlike root directory, sub directories can be created and renamed. These directories can be given any name. As a standard, some unix systems follow the naming convention as

For example

/dev :-Directory to store special files used to represent real physical devices such as terminals and printers
/var :-Directory under which all log files are organized in some systems
/temp :-This is a directory that acts as a scratching pad and contains all temporary files.
/etc :- Directory contains various configuration and command files
/bin :- Directory to store unix utilities

What is HOME directory on Unix

HOME directory is a directory like any other subdirectory under root directory in Unix file system. However this has a special significance in unix operating system.

Whenever you log in to unix operating system you are placed in a directory called "home" directory. This home directory would have been assigned to you by system administrator while setting up your account in the system. If you create any files they get stored in your "home" directory, unless you change your working directory. So by default your "home" directory becomes your working directory.

Unix being a multi-user operating system, all users would have been setup to have their own "home" directory when their account is created in the unix operating system. As mentioned previously Unix file system is well organized and it makes perfectly sense to have all users "home" directories under a sub directory called /home under root file system.

```
 /  (root)
 -------------
 |       |
/home   /tmp
```

Every users "home" directory would have a unique sub directory under /home directory to separate individual users from landing in the same directory when they login.

For example

If you have a userid called "oracle" your "home" directory would look like /home/oracle
you can create files and sub directories under your "home" (/home/oracle) directory.

So "home" directory is the sub directory (/home/oracle) you are placed in immediately after you login to the system.

How to navigate to other sub directories

First time when you login to unix operating system, you are placed in your "home" directory. You can find out the actual listing of the subdirectories by executing the command pwd

pwd

/home/oracle

pwd :- stands for present working directory.

You can create sub directories under /home/oracle. And to navigate to newly created directory say "john" you use cd command

cd john

pwd
/home/oracle/john

If you want to navigate back to /home/oracle (one level up) you use the command

cd ..

Instead if you want to navigate from /home/oracle/john to /home directory (two levels up) you could use the command
cd ../..

You can always use **full pathname** to take you anywhere in the file system

For example

To navigate from /home/oracle/john   to   /usr/programs/tmp directory use the command

cd /usr/programs/tmp

Irrespective of your pwd (present working directory) location, using **full pathname** will take you to the directory you mentioned in the path

Unix file system being a huge file system, you may often end up working in various subdirectories, and you may have to return to your "home" directory. Return to your home sweet home. In unix operating system there is a special command to take you to your "home" directory irrespective of your present working directory. Typing just cd will place you back in your "home" directory

cd

pwd
/home/oracle
How about if you want to navigate to other users home directory in unix file system. There is special character called tilde (~) which can be used to navigate to other users home directory. However this character usage is available on few shells such as Korn, C and BASH

For example:-

If you want to navigate from your current working directory to oracle9   user's "home" directory

cd ~oracle9

This command will place you in /home/oracle9 directory.

Access permission on files and directories

When you create files and directories you have full permission to read write and execute these files and you become the owner of these files. By default all other users on the unix system do not have the right to read, write and execute files created by other users.

To display the access permission on any file or directory use the command

ls –l filename
ls –l directory name

-rwxr--r-- 1 oracle oinstall   748 Dec 4 2008 setenv

From file or directory ownership point of view unix classifies any user under three categories

user :- Normally any user who owns the file
group :- Users who belong to the same group as the owner
others :- Rest of the users

Depending on the access permission any file or directory would have three flags

r read permission
w write permission
x execute permission

The access permissions can be represented by nine characters for all three types of user as follows

user   group others
 r w x   r w x   r w x

Following file "setenv" has read, write and execute permission to user. Read permission to group users and read permission to other users.

-rwxr--r-- 1 oracle oinstall 748 Dec 4 2008 setenv

As an owner of the file when you create a new file it's access permissions are set to default.

What if you want to change the permission on any given file or directory you created. Before that it is important you understand how the permissions work on unix file system.

Access permission on the file or directory you just created depends on the "file creation mask". In unix operating system there is something called file creation mask represented by "umask". This simply consists of three octal digits.

Whenever you create a file or directory it creates files with permission 666 and directories with permission 777 by default. However if umask value is set, this value would be subtracted from actual permission count

For example

umask value is set to 066
System value for directories 777
Default access permission (777 –066) ➔711

The created directory by default would look like
rwxrw-rw-
(7 1 1)

To display current value of umask just type

umask

To set new value for umask

umask nnn (n represents any value between 0 and 7)

So as a owner whenever you create new files or directories, the default access permission is determined by "umask" value.

The permission numbers on files and directories are represented by octal numbers. mask permissions also based on octal numbers

Octal number   Permission access

0	rwx	read, write and execute
1	rw-	read and write
2	r-x	read and execute
3	r--	read only
4	-wx	write and execute
5	-w-	write only
6	--x	execute only
7	---	no permissions

Chapter 5
Permission and security with Files and Directories

Unix system security

Why Security ?

Unix system needs to be protected for it's valuable content. Computer systems are used to store, process and report valuable information. Having said that it is important you take care of your relevant data.

Unix system security is applicable in various levels. As an oracle dba you need to take care of security in following level

- User access level (Password protection)
- File permission
- Directory permission

Every user on a Unix system has a unique username, and is a member of at least one group (the primary group for that user). This group information is held in the password file (/etc/passwd). A user can also be a member of one or more other groups. The auxiliary group information is held in the file /etc/group. Only the administrator can create new groups or add/delete group members (one of the shortcomings of the system).

Most of the Unix Security is taken care by Unix system administrator. However your account for database need to be protected by using the secure password practices.

One of the important part of security is the file and directory permission

Chapter 5: Permission and security with Files and Directories

File Permission

As discussed in chapter 4 of this book, when you create files and directories you have full permission to read write and execute these files and you become the owner of these files. By default all other users on the unix system do not have the right to read, write and execute files created by other users.

Every directory and file on the system has an owner, and also an associated group. It also has a set of permission flags which specify separate read, write and execute permissions for the 'user' (owner), 'group', and 'other' (everyone else with an account on the computer)

From file or directory ownership point of view unix classifies any user under three categories

user :- Normally any user who owns the file
group :- Users who belong to the same group as the owner
others :- Rest of the users

Depending on the access permission any file or directory would have three flags

r read permission
w write permission
x execute permission

The access permissions can be represented by nine characters for all three types of user as follows

The three user categories are

> The file's owner
> Members of the same Unix group as the file's owner

> ➢ All other Unix users.

user   group   others
r w x   r w x   r w x

The file permissions are represented by numeric values.

For example

-rwxr-xr-- 1 oracle oinstall   0 Aug 31 15:25 fd

The above file has permission level set to 754

7 represents user access level (read, write and execute) permission.

5 represents group access level (read and execute)

4 represents other access level (read only)

The Numeric values with permission access for files and directories are as follows

Numeric value   Permission access

7   rwx read, write and execute
6   rw- read and write
5   r-x read and execute
4   r-- read only
3   -wx write and execute
2   -w- write only
1   --x execute only
0   ---   no permissions

umask

Each user has a default set of permissions which apply to all files created by that user. The default file permission for any given user is set by system administrator and often inherited from login process. However file permission set on any file or directory can be controlled by modifying the value of "umask"

"umask" is user file-creation mode mask. It can be used to control the default file permission for new files. "umask" is represented by four-digit octal number.

You can find out the default system permission setting for your userid by temporarily resetting the umask value to 000 .

For example

1. create a file and check the permission

   $ touch tmp

   $ ls -l tmp

-rw-r--r-- 1 oracle   oinstall   0 Sep 1 08:15 tmp

The file tmp got created with permission (644)

2. unset the value of umask to 000

   $umask   000

3. create a file and check permission

   $ls -l temp1

-rw-rw-rw- 1 oracle   oinstall   0 Sep 1 08:19 temp1

The file temp1 got created with file permission (666)

To change the file permission on any file or directory you own, you could use "chmod" command

For example

$chmod 755 temp1

$ ls -l temp1

-rwxr-xr-x 1 oracle oinstall   0 Sep 1 08:44 temp1

Note:- The umask setting affects only new files as they are created. It does not affect permissions on existing files. umask command needs to be run every time you log on. Having said that it would be ideal to place umask command in .profile

set new value for umask

umask nnn (n represents any value between 0 and 7)
"umask" is represented by four-digit octal number and the octal values are as follows

Octal number	Permission access
0	rwx read, write and execute
1	rw- read and write
2	r-x read and execute
3	r-- read only
4	-wx write and execute
5	-w- write only
6	--x execute only
7	--- no permissions

As a owner whenever you create a file or directory, the permissions on these files and directory is determined by 2 parameters

1. System values set on file and directory for a given user
2. umask value

System values:- Every time a userid is created by system administrator, userid would be assigned a specific file permission setting.

umask value:- "umask" is user file-creation mode mask. It is represented by four-digit octal number.

The actual file or directory permission is determined as follows

For example

System value for directories 777
umask value is set to 066
Default access permission on new directories created by user
(777 –066) -> **711**

System value for files 666
umask value is set to 066
Default access permission on new files created by user (666 – 066) -> **600**

The created new directory by default would have read, write and execute permission to user, execute permission to group and others as follows.
drwx--x--x
(7   1   1)

The created new file by default would have read and execute permission to user, and no permissions granted to group and others as follows.

-rw-------

(600)

To display current value of umask just type

umask

In summary:

Whenever you create a file or directory it creates files with permission 666 and directories with permission 777 by default. However if umask value is set, this value would be subtracted from actual permission count.

Part 3

Chapter 6
Managing Jobs and
processes

What is a process

Basically a program in execution is called process. When you enter a command it invokes program. Though you have a single copy of given program stored in your file system, you could execute the program multiple times in any given time and you could have multiple processes out of single program.

Each and every process on unix system is identified by unique process ID. On unix system any command you enter at the command prompt turns out to be a process.

For example

When you first login to the system, your shell program gets started and it is identified by a unique process and process id. Every process started within the shell has it's own unique process id and they are called sub processes.

How to list processes

If you enter the command "ps" at your command prompt, it would list all processes owned by you (your userid) and processes associated with your terminal.

For example

 $ps

```
 PID TTY       TIME CMD
 1034 pts/19    0:00 ps
 7618 pts/19    0:00 ksh
```

"ps" command has number of options and the usage of these options depends on whether you use System V or BSD

To display all process belong to your userid (oracle), type following command

For example

On System V

ps –u oracle

PID TTY	TIME CMD
14582 ?	41:09 emagent
23848 ?	41:48 oracle
19026 ?	0:01 sshd
23811 ?	0:17 oracle
3932 pts/19	0:00 ps
23817 ?	0:32 oracle
7618 pts/19	0:00 ksh
24046 ?	0:04 oracle
23821 ?	0:46 oracle
4713 pts/17	0:00 ksh

On BSD

ps –x

If you like to display information about other users on the system

For example you like to get the information about user called "oracle9i"

On System V

ps –u oracle9i

On BSD

ps –aux|grep oracle9i

On BSD system "ps –aux" command lists a table of processes, arranged in order of decreasing CPU usage when the ps –aux command is executed. This display is often useful to get most active processes:

Display Unix Processes

The basic process management command is the ps command. It is commonly used to display active processes and their characteristics.

On BSD

Sps -aux | head –5

```
USER     PID %CPU %MEM  SZ RSS TTY STAT  TIME COMMAND
oracle   12923 74.2 22.5 223 376 p5  R    2:12 f77 -o ora_Instal.sh
oracle9i 16725 10.9 50.8 1146 1826 p6  R N 56:04 g94 sql.dat
oracle   17026 3.5 1.2 354 240 co  I   0:19 vi oracle.txt
susan    7997 0.2 0.3 142 46 p3  S   0:04 csh
```

Some of the interesting column headings from "**ps –aux**" represent the following

USER Username of process owner.
PID Process ID.
%CPU Estimated fraction of CPU consumed (BSD).
%MEM Estimated fraction of system memory consumed (BSD).
SZ Virtual memory used in K (BSD) or pages (System V).
RSS Real memory used (in same units as SZ).
TTY Terminal port associated with process.
STAT Current process state (BSD);
TIME:- Time spent by the command/process
COMMAND: Command/program run by the user

The first line of this output shows that user oracle is running a shell program (ora_Instal.sh). This process has PID   12923 and is currently either running or run able. User oracle9i process (PID 16725), executing the program g94, is also running or run able, though at a lowered priority.

The most important column to watch for would be %CPU and %MEM for any given user

From above display, it's obvious that most system resources are used by oracle and oracle9i processes .
Oracle and oracle9i have about 85% of the CPU and 73% of the memory between them.

On System V

ps –ef|grep ora

```
UID    PID PPID  C  STIME  TTY    TIME  CMD
oracle  484 15014  0  Sep 07   ?       45:14 ora_mmnl_test
oracle  4383 15014  0 09:10:20  ?        0:00 oracletest (LOCAL=NO)
oracle 23747 15014  0  Sep 05   ?        0:34 ora_dbw0_test2
```

The column definitions that you should be aware of are

UID: The user ID that owns the process.
PID: The process ID for the task
PPID: The parent process.
STIME: The start time of the process.
TIME: The amount of CPU time used by the process so far. This value keep increasing until the process is complete
CMD: The unix command that is being executed.

At any given moment of time Unix system would normally be running number of processes. Every command you enter at the command prompt turns into a process while under execution.

If you run a unix built in command, it executes in the shell's own process. However if you run a non- built in command, shell forks a new process (child process) to run the command. So when non built-in command gets executed, you have a parent process (your shell) waiting for the child process to complete. Parent process gets reactivated only when child process dies and shell prompt returns.

What is a foreground process

Any process started by a built-in command or non built-in command , that engages your command prompt until all child processes and parent process dies. If your foreground process is been running for very long time and for whatever reason you wish to cancel this process, you could do so by entering Ctrl-c (Hold down the key marked Ctrl and press C key on your keyboard).   This interrupt would cancel your process and return the command prompt.

If you wish to suspend the foreground job you could do so by entering Ctrl-z
Once you suspend any process, you have 2 options. Either you terminate the process and restart the job later. Most of the shells except Bourne shell gives you the option of restarting the process, however on Bourne shell, once you suspend the job you may have to terminate using kill command.

What is a background process

Suppose you need to run a long process, say rman backup script (rman_bkp.sh) on one of your big database. You know that this job is going to run for several minutes and you do not wish to engage your terminal/command prompt. You could choose to run this script in the background mode.

To run process in the background as a job/command, enter the command as follows

$rman_bkp.sh &

As we discussed in previously, unix system assigns a process ID number for every job/process it runs.

Process Id on Unix system

Any process when gets created on unix, shell assigns a processes number called process ID. This process ID is a unique number assigned to individual processes. All unix processes are identified by their Process Id's (PID). They are called process identification numbers.

Whenever you run a command in the background by appending & to it, the shell forks a child process to run the command responds with a line that looks like this:

$rman_bkp.sh &
[1]   7326

Process Job number on Unix

In this example 7326 is the process ID for the   process "rman_bkp.sh". The [1] is a job number assigned by the shell (not the operating system).

Note:- Job numbers refers to background processes that are currently running under your shell, while process Ids refer to all processes currently running on the entire system, for all users.

If you start up additional background jobs while the first one is still running, the shell will number them 2 , 3 etc For example;

$ cmd1 &
[2]   8756
$ cmd2 &
[3]   2221

The shell includes job numbers in messages it prints when a background job completes, like this;

[1]   + Done   rman_bkp.sh &

Advantage of submitting jobs in background mode

A foreground job can receive keyboard input and signals such as Control-C from the controlling terminal, whereas background jobs cannot. If the login session is disconnected, foreground jobs are terminated by a hang-up signal, while background jobs are not. Both foreground and background jobs can write to the controlling terminal.

Jobs can be submitted in the background and foreground depending on the convenience. Jobs can also be swapped between foreground and background mode on almost all shells except Bourne shell.

How to switch process between background and foreground

To place a foreground process in the background

1. First suspend the foreground job by entering Ctrl-z
2. Enter bg (background) command to move suspended process into the background.

3. Enter fg (foreground) command if you wish to restart the process in foreground mode.

To place a background process in the foreground

1. Enter fg(foreground) command followed by the job number
   fg   job_number

Note:- If there is only one background job running on your system, you don't have to pass the parameter "job_number" to "**fg**" command. Instead just enter fg

   fg

How to list all active background processes

Because background processes run in the background, it would not be visible at your command prompt to know if a given job is active or not.

To list all background processes running on the unix system, use "jobs" command

run.sh &
[3]   23197

jobs

[3] + Running   run.sh &
[2] – Stopped   rman_bkp.sh &
[1]   Running   cmd1.sh &

jobs -l

[3] + 23197   Running   run.sh &

```
[2] - 22784   Stopped        rman_bkp.sh &
[1]   22573   Running        cmd1.sh  &
```

jobs -p
23197
22784
22573

"**jobs**" command displays the job number, its state and job/command associated with it.
"**jobs –l**" command also displays process ID associated with each job.
"**jobs –p**" command lists only Process Ids

Control Key signals in Unix

Previously in this chapter we observed that entering "Ctrl -c" stops any foreground job. Likewise "Ctrl -z" suspends the job. In both scenario, system has responded to some kind of signal and acted accordingly.

Ctrl –c (control – c) sends interrupt signal to current job. Ctrl –z (control – z) sends terminal stop signal. Likewise Ctrl-\ (control-backslash) sends QUIT signal to current job.

Ctrl -\ signal is a stronger version of Ctrl –c and you normally don't attempt this unless Ctrl –c doesn't work.

In summary

CTRL-C → Interrupt Signal
CTRL-Z → Terminal Stop Signal
CTRL-\ → Quit Signal

How to kill process

Sometimes you may encounter situations where a given process turns out to be high resource consuming one, taking longer time than expected to complete and you may wish to terminate the process. To terminate the process/job use "kill" command.

To kill a particular job, first you need to identify the Process ID associated with job using "ps" command

kill   process id

kill command sends different signals to the system based on the options used with kill command

kill process id   :- Sends a simple cancel signal just like Ctrl –c and it cancels the process

kill –1 process id :- This signals the process to hang up just like you logging out. System attempts to kill any child process.

kill –9 process id :- This is used as a last resort and it will stop any process dead, however it may leave any child processes still running.

Part 4

Chapter 7
Unix Shell

What is Unix Shell

Unix shell is a command -line interpreter. unix shell is also called command programming language. This command programming language provides an interface to the unix operating system. Basically unix shell is programming language, command language and also provides an interface to the Unix operating system.

When you login to your system you are basically placed in a program. This program greets you with the prompt. This very program is shell.

The command prompt is a character at the start of the command –line. Whenever you see a prompt, that is an indication that shell is ready to receive your command. By default this character is $ (dollar sign) or % (percent sign). However this command prompt character can be customized (more on this customization in later chapters)

Shell acts as a command interpreter, that means every command you enter at the command prompt, shell passes it to operating system kernel. Unix operating system kernel acts upon the command, process it and control is passed back to shell. Shell finally displays the results of the operation on your screen.

Apart from interpreting your command, shell does lot more. When you type a command and it doesn't exists in your current working directory, shell searches this command in other proper directories. Shell interprets command –line wildcards and it also takes care of your environment customization.

Chapter 7: Unix Shell

The beauty of unix operating system is, it supports multiple shells. Each shell has it's unique feature, though most of the comamnds and the way it carries out task is similar. Normally unix operating system comes with multiple shells and you could choose which shell you would like to play with.

Type of shells

Generally most unix systems aware of at least three shells: the Bourne shell (**sh**), the C shell (**csh**) and the most popular one Korn shell (**ksh**).

Any shell itself is a program and you can execute any shell like any other program

When you first login you would be placed in one of the available shell depending on your profile (more on profile in later chapters). However you can switch between shells.

For example

To switch to Korn shell (ksh), just type "**ksh**" at your prompt

ksh

To switch to C shell (csh) just type "**csh**" at your prompt

csh

To switch to Bourne shell (sh) just type "**sh**" at your prompt

sh

Only disadvantage of having the support of multiple shells on unix system is, sometimes you may have shell scripts written in C shell (csh) and when you try to execute them under Korn shell (ksh) or Bourne shell (sh), you may encounter errors. To avoid this, it would be a wise practice to always specify script's shell in the script itself by special comment

For example include the following line as first line of your script based on the type of shell (csh, ksh, sh etc)

#! /bin/csh

#! /bin/ksh

#! /bin/sh

If you specify the type of shell by using this special comment in every shell script, even if you run the script in incorrect shell, current shell will spawn the correct shell type and execute the script.

Bourne shell (sh)

Bourne shell used to be the default unix shell in older version of unix and it is the orginal shell, written by Steve Bourne from Bell labs. Though it is the original shell type and available on almost all unix system, it has few limitation. Few shell features shuch as command alias, command line editing and command history are not available on bourne.

Korn shell (ksh)

It is developed in early 1980's by David Korn from AT&T Bell Laboratories. It provides all features of C and TC shell, it is backward compatible with bourne shell. Korn shell is quite popular and you normally find quite a lot of scripts written in Korn shell. It is used as a programming language on Unix.

Bash shell

It is the part of GNU project written by Free software foundation. Bash shell is also called Bourne again shell (bash). The advantage of bash shell is, it provides all interactive features of Korn shell (ksh), C shell (csh). It is also considered as a programming language on unix.

Bash is the shell for the GNU operating system. Bash shell can be run on most of the unix-like operating system. This shell is most popular among academic community.

C shell

C shell scripting syntax is modeled after the C programming language and that is how it got it's name C shell. C shell was originally designed for BSD unix system. C shell is not very widely used on unix.

Your working environment in Unix

As we discussed already unix provides wide range of environment and choices to work with. Based on the type of user and requirement, you could alter this environment by customization.

Whenever you login to unix system, you are placed in one of the shell. However your working environment within this shell is determined by the values set in the initialization file, which is always read before you are greeted with shell prompt upon login. The environment values are set using variables in initialization file. These values can always be changed by editing the file.

Some of the variables are as follows:-

PATH : This variable lists the directories for the shell to look through to find a command

For example

PATH=/usr/bin:/opt/oracle/product/10.2.4/bin:/etc:/sbin:/bin

These directories are searched in the order in which they appear.

SHELL: Sets your default shell.

HISTFILE: Name of the history file, on which the editing modes operate

EDITOR: Pathname of your favourite text editor.

MAILPATH: List of filenames, separated by colons (to check for incoming mail)

MAIL: Name of the file to check for information mail.

Some of the variables may vary depending on the type of shell you are using. To check which shell you are currently using, type

echo $SHELL

The above command will display the full path of the shell you are currently using.

For example this command displays one of the output depending on the type of shell. The full path of the shell may vary from system to system.

/bin/ksh	Korn shell
/bin/sh	Bourne shell
/bin/bash	Bash shell
/bin/csh	C shell

Your unix environment file

Your working environment values are set in the variables and are basically sourced from two files on most of unix systems. First file is **/etc/profile** and the second file is **$HOME/.profile**

The /etc/profile is a system wide environment file that contains system wide environment settings and also startup programs. Since this file contains system wide environment settings, it also applies to entire system and all users on the system.

$HOME/.profile contrary to /etc/profile file, is user preferred configuration file for configuring user environment. Every user will have their own environment file, normally called **.profile** located in "home" directory of individual user. The naming convention may slightly vary based on the shell you are using. You can change your own .profile file and add/edit additional environment setting and further customize your environment.

The /etc/profile file would be run every time the system gets re-booted and when you login all the variables set in the $HOME/.profile file will be executed and your environment would be ready with the settings in your profile file.

What if you wish to set some additional environment variables ?. You could do this by using

set *variable_name=value*
or
export *variable_name=value*

Depending on the type of shell you are using. First syntax is applicable for C shell and TC shell whereas second syntax is applicable for Bourne shell, Korn shell and bash shell

Any changes made at the command prompt using above method would last only as long as your login session is active. What if you want this change to be a permanent change and would like to have every time you login.

You can do a permanent change in your environment by adding/editing the **$HOME/.profile** file.

You can also execute **$HOME/.profile** file at any time within your session to source the changes you just added in this file

Chapter 8

Unix Environment and Command line

What is a command

When you login to unix system you would be placed in the shell and greeted with shell prompt. This is an indication that unix system is ready for you to enter any commands. A command on UNIX is something you enter at the shell prompt to interact with Unix operating system. Shell prompt is also called command prompt because that is where you enter your commands.

The basic command would have three components. Command name, options and arguments. However second and third components are optional.

The general syntax of command is

Command_name options argument(s)

For example

$date
Friday, 4 September 2009 3:48:44 PM EST

Above is a simple command without any options and arguments. This command displays date with full format.

Why options ?

Sometime you may wish to have variations in the output of any command

For example

$date %Y
2009

Above command has an option called "%Y". Because of this option, the output of the date command has changed from full version to only "2009", that is only year is displayed.

Options modify the way that a command works.

What is command arguments ?

Arguments work differently from options. When options modify the way command works, arguments are passed to commands as mandatory entities. Some commands work without arguments, however some commands must have arguments for the command to work.

For example

$date
Friday, 4 September 2009 3:48:44 PM EST

Above command "**date**" does not require any argument for successful execution.

$cp file1   file2

In above example "cp" command needs two arguments "file1" and "file2" for it's successful execution. If you don't pass the arguments "**cp**" command would fail.

Some time depending on the command, options and arguments your command line could exceed more than a line. It makes perfectly sense to remember this lengthy command line by another short name. Unix has a facility called "command alias"

Command Alias

In general "command alias" is a command in various shells on unix such as Korn shell, C shell, bash shell etc, which enables a replacement for another command or command line

If you use a command with options, arguments regularly and this command line is a comprehensive refined string to perform certain task, it completely makes sense to replace this string with "command alias"

How to create command alias

The syntax to create "command alias" varies depending on the shell you use.

For example

In Korn shell the syntax would be

alias *alias_name*=definition_of_alias

Following command line lists all files with extension ".log" older than 2 days in current directory

$find . -name "*.log" -mtime +2
./redirected_restore.log
./listbkp.log
./sqlnet.log

If we have to create an alias for the above command line it would look like

alias list_logs='find . -name "*.log" -mtime +2'

To execute the above command line you execute the alias name and in this example it is "list_logs", which would list all the files with extension "*.log" and older than 2 days in current directory.

$ list_logs

./redirected_restore.log

./listbkp.log

./sqlnet.log

Note:- In case of alias the underlying command line is executed every time you execute the alias.

Command alias can be referred to another alias. That is alias within an alias

For example

alias **list_logs**='find . -name "*.log" -mtime +2'

alias **page_log**='cd /tmp/log; ls –ltr | **list_logs**'

In above example we created a first command alias called "**list_logs**" and we referred this alias within second command line to create another alias called "**page_log**"

Though concept of "command alias" is to get around the command lines quicker and help remember the comprehensive command syntax, what if we forget the name of the alias itself already defined in your current shell

There is a command on unix to display all defined "command aliases" known to your shell. If you type "alias" at your shell/command prompt, it would list all aliases known to your shell.

For example

$alias

bdf='df -k'
dbs='cd $ORACLE_HOME/dbs;pwd;ls'
em='cd /pkgs/oracle/product/oracle/EM;pwd;ls -l'
functions='typeset -f'
history='fc -l'
initora='cd $ORACLE_HOME/dbs;more init$ORACLE_SID.ora'
integer='typeset -i'
l='ls -l|pg'
net9='cd $ORACLE_HOME/network/admin;pwd;ls'
oba='cd $ORACLE_BASE/admin/$ORACLE_SID;pwd;ls'
oback='cd /data/backup/rman_backups/$ORACLE_SID;pwd;ls'
oexp='cd /data/backup/exports/$ORACLE_SID;pwd;ls -lt'
oh='cd $ORACLE_HOME;pwd;ls'
otars='cd /data/back/tars/$ORACLE_SID;pwd;ls -lt'

To display the current value of a given alias use the command

alias alias_name

To cancel a command alias use the command

unalias alias_name

Note:- If you would like to define a "command alias" and use it every time when you login, add the command alias definition line within **.profile** file. Every time you login .profile file would be executed and your current environment would be defined with this alias.

Chapter 8: Unix Environment and Command line

Shell Variables

Any unix process runs in a specific environment. Environment consists of number of environment variables.

Variable is a way of passing information from the shell to programs when you run them. Programs look "in the environment" for particular variables and if they are found will use the values stored. Some are set by the system, others by you, yet others by the shell, or any program that loads another program.

On unix shell maintains a set of internal variables and these variables are called *shell variables*. These shell variables are responsible for the shell to work in a particular way. shell variables apply only to the current instance of the shell and are used to set short-term working conditions. they are not available to the parent or child shells. In general shell variable names are defined in lower case in the C shell family and upper case in the Bourne shell family.

Shell variables are defined using following syntax

On C Shell family

A shell variable is defined by the "set" command and deleted by the "unset" command.

To set the shell variable

% set shell_var_name=*value*

To un set the shell variable

% unset shell_var_name

To display the value of shell variable

% echo $shell_var_name

On Korn Shell family

The syntax to set shell variables on Korn shell family is slightly different. However the syntax to unset and display the shell variable remains same.

To set the shell variable

$export shell_var_name=*value*

Note:- Do not leave spaces around the equal sign (=).

To un set the shell variable

$unset shell_var_name

To display the value of shell variable

$echo $shell_var_name

Environment variable

Unix system maintains a second category of variables along with shell variables and these variables are called "environment variables". Technically environment variables are not confined to current shell session, rather they are set at login. When you login to unix system they get defined by the "env" file and available to your current shell session. If you run any process, these variables would be available for the current process and will be passed on to child processes as well.

Some of the environment variables on Unix are as follows:

PATH :- This variable defines the list of directories searched for executable files. whenever you type a command in Unix shell

PWD :-   Your current directory

HISTFILE :- Name of the history file, on which the editing modes operate

EDITOR :- Pathname of your favourite text editor, the suffix (macs or vi) determines which   editing mode to use

USER :-   Username of a Unix user

TERM :- Terminal or terminal emulator used by a current user

MAIL:- Name of the file to check for information mail. (i.e your mail file)

HOME :- Full path to a user's home directory

Prompting Variables

When you login to Unix system you would be placed in the shell and shell displays a command/shell prompt. When you see this prompt, this is an indication that unix system is ready yo accept your command. The default command prompt for root user is # and for rest of the users it is $ (dollar sign)

However shell's prompt is not engraved in stone and users do change it to something else for their own convenience.

Shell has a variable called "PS1" which stands for "prompting string 1". This variable stores the value of your command prompt or shell prompt. In simple terms, if you wish to change your prompting string, you simply change the value of variable "PS1". This prompt is called primary prompt.

For example:- You could set your own user id as the primary prompting string.

PS1="($LOGNAME)->"

(oracle)->

In above example your login user id is "oracle" and "LOGNAME" is built-in shell variable in unix shell, which is set to your login name when you log in. When you execute the above statement your prompt gets changed to "(oracle)->".

You could substitute with any value for your primary prompt string.

Sometimes when you are working within the file system and deeply embedded in file system branches, you might feel that you are lost. Situations like this, it may be very useful to set your current working directory as your primary prompting string. This will enable you to know where you are at any time when you are working on unix system, without typing "**pwd**" to remember where you are.

However the present working directory keeps changing, as you navigate from one directory to another and one file system to another. Having said that we need to substitute the value of variable "PS1" is such a way that it re-valuates the content every time you change the directory. This re-valuation process can be achieved by using single quotes, instead of double quotes, surrounding the string on the right side of the assignment as follows.

PS1='($PWD) --> '

For example:

PS1='($PWD)->'

(/home/oracle)->

 (/home/oracle)->cd –

(/home/oracle/prog/bin/backup/log)->

In above example the moment I enter "**cd –**" command, the prompt got changed from "**(/home/oracle)->**" to "**(/home/oracle/prog/bin/backup/log)->**"

Secondary Prompt

You might have noticed when you type an incomplete line and hit RETURN, at your primary prompt, the shell will display a secondary prompt and wait for you to complete the command and hit enter again. This secondary prompt by default is indicated by character >

This secondary prompt also can be customized according to your taste and convenient just like primary prompt. Secondary prompt is stored in a variable called **PS2** and you can change the secondary prompt string by changing the value of this variable.

Unix shell also has two more additional prompting variables called **PS3** and **PS4** and they are used in shell programming and debugging

File search path

PATH is an environment variable on unix system. When you type in a command shell tries to identify/search your command in certain directory list, and this directory search is determined by the content of the variable **PATH.** The **PATH** variable helps shell to find the command you enter at the command prompt. This variable has a list of directories that the shell searches every time you enter a command; the directory names are separated by colons :

For example, if you type **print $PATH**, you will see something like this:

/sbin:/usr/sbin:/usr/bin:/etc:/usr/ucb:/local/bin

Suppose you have created a directory say **/home/you/bin** for your own shell scripts. To add this directory to your **PATH,** append this directory to existing directory string as follows

PATH=$PATH:/home/you/bin

Sometime it is not possible to remember the location of a particular executable or utility. There is a command in unix which gives the location of a command or utility or executable and it is called **"whence"** command. The **whence** command is a Korn Shell feature.

This is the command which gives the location of a command. The **whence** command tells how a name would be interpreted by the shell: whence command detects commands, utilities and aliases by searching your path.

If you need to know which directory a command comes from, you need not look at directories in your **PATH** until you find it. The shell built-in command **whence** prints the full pathname of the command you give it as argument, or just the command's name.

For example

$whence exp
/opt/oracle/product/10.2.4/bin/exp

Above command list the directory location of the "exp" utility

Directory Search Path

Just like the definition of **PATH** variable, there is an another user defined variable in unix which enables you to define the search path for directories. This search path is defined with a variable called "**CDPATH**"

PATH variable helps to locate the file location, where as **CDPATH** helps to locate the directory location.

When you type cd command, **CDPATH** environment variable defines additional locations to be searched.

For example

When you type **cd A**, cd will look for **A** in the current directory. If you define the **CDPATH** environment variable which consists of a list of directories, **cd** will look for **A** in the current directory and if it is not found, the search continues in the directories defined in **CDPATH**, from left to right, stopping at the first place where it is found. Your working directory is then switched to **A**.

CDPATH is a variable whose value, like that of PATH, is a list of directories separated by colons. Its purpose is to augment the functionality of the **cd** built-in command. By default, CDPATH is not set, that means CDPATH value is set to null be default. When you type **cd** dirname, the shell will look in the current directory for a subdirectory called dirname.

Unix Environment File

Your unix environment basically consists of number of customization in terms of variables, alias etc. If you have to maintain this customisation for all the processes you run in your session, it is worth storing these setting somewhere in a file and run them every time you login. This helps to maintain a consistency of your environment.

There is a special file in unix called environment file just to store all required variable, aliases etc. You can store this file anywhere in the file system, however you need to set the environment variable "ENV" to identify this location

Environmental file sets up the user environment. Though environment variables are usually known to sub processes, the shell must be explicitly told which other variables, options, aliases, etc, are to be communicated to sub processes. Any miscellaneous variables, alias etc can be put in a special file called the environment file.

We know that **.profile** file gets executed every time user logs into the system. So call this environment file within the .profile

You can call the environment file anything you like, as long as you set the environment variable **ENV** to the file's name. The usual way to do this is as follows:

- Choose a filename to include all your definitions you wish to propagate to subprocesses and add them to this file.
- set the environment variable "ENV" to identify this file location
- Include a line in your .profile to indicate the Environment file.
        ENV=Envfilename
- Execute .profile for the changes to take place
        . profile

It is a good practice to put as few definitions as possible in **.profile** and as many as possible in your environment file.

Chapter 9

Unix Shell and Programming

What is Unix Command line?

Unix commands and command lines you enter at the shell prompt/command prompt may vary depending on type of command or command line. It is possible to make mistakes when you type at a computer keyboard. All unix shells offer with many ways of editing the command line.

Command-line editing can be helpful whenever the number of keystrokes it takes you to edit and re-run a command is less than the number of keystrokes to re-type it.
To enable command-line editing, you need to set few variables depending on the type of shell you are using.

Command line editing is done using the same keystrokes as the editors. For example emacs, gmacs or vi (more on vi editor in later chapters).

For example

If you set the variable EDITOR to vi, you would be using the same keystrokes during command-line editing as you would use in vi editing.

BASH and Korn Shell

The environment variables EDITOR or/and VISUAL needs to be set in BASH and Korn Shell. This can be emacs, gmacs or vi. This is applicable for both Korn and bash shell.

EDITOR=vi

Note:-If you set VISUAL variable, this value takes precedence over EDITOR variable.

You can also turn on the command-line editing by using shell command to set an option and this is done using command.

To set emacs editor

set —o emacs

or

To set vi editor

set —o vi

How to create commands and programs

Unix shell has number of built-in commands which can be used to carry out it's intended functionality. Unix shell also facilitates grouping of built-in commands into a file and execute them as a program. This is called a shell script. All shell scripts can be executed just like commands in unix shell.

Unix shell in general provides a programming environment. Unix operating system along with Unix shell provides a flexible set of simple tools to allow you to perform a wide variety of system-management, text-processing, and general-purpose tasks. These simple tools can be used in very powerful ways by tying them together programmatically, using "shell scripts" or "shell programs".

Programming syntax may slightly vary depending on which shell you are using as command interpreter.

Bourne shell scripts also work under the bash (Bourne Again Shell) shell. Bourne shell is compatible with Korn shell. The

C and TC shells use a programming language which is similar to the C programming language.
Hundred miles journey starts with the first step.

Shell script

To create simple shell script, put command lines into a file and set the execute permission on the file and execute it.

- Shell scripts are simple text files created with an editor.
- Shell scripts are executable files

Simple shell script has some basic building blocks

For example

cat sample.sh

#!/bin/sh

\#   This is a simple script to display   username,   current working directory and Today's date

echo "My username is : `who am i` \n"

echo "My current working directory is:"

pwd

echo

echo "Todays date is : \c"

date

In the above simple shell script

The first line indicates explicitly the type of shell (#!), this script would be running. It is a good practice to indicate the type of shell the script is meant to be executing.

The second and third lines beginning with a hash (**#**) are comments and are not interpreted by the shell.

"echo" command is used to display any string or value of any variable

The backquotes (`) around the command "who am i" are used as command substitution.

pwd, date and who am i are simple built-in shell commands

\c informs the shell to stay on the same line

\n informs the shell to add an extra carriage return.

You can create a shell script using the text editor of your choice. when you create a file with a text editor, the file is set up with read and write permission for you and read-only permission for everyone else.

Therefore you must give your script execute permission explicitly, by using the chmod command

chmod +x sample.sh

Since shell scripts are made up of shell commands and all these commands are interpreted by the shell, having said that shell scripts are executable files.
To execute the shell script simply type script name

For example

sample.sh

If your script is not in current working directory, you could indicate the shell to search in your directories set in "PATH" variable and still execute it by typing

./sample.sh

When you execute the script by just typing the name (first method), shell spawns another copy of shell called subshell and runs the script as a sub process. Once the subshell executes the commands in the script, it gets terminated and the control is handled back to the parent shell.

Well what happens when you execute this shell script in background.

For example

sample.sh &

When you append "&" to the end of the script, it runs in background, and once again this whole script is executed within a subprocess.

You can also execute this script by typing

. sample.sh

In this method the script runs in the same shell

Unix shell provides perfect programming environment like any other language. Since unix supports multiple shells, you have the flexibility of writing script in different shell and still make it executable in the same unix operating system

Variables as place holders

In any programming language one of the main feature is the ability to define and assign values to variables to store information.

Variable name can begin with a letter upper or lower case, underscore or even with the number.

How to assign values to variables

Values are assigned to shell variables using assignment operator = as follows

varname=100

In above example value 100 is assigned to variable name "varname". Note that no embedded spaces are allowed before and after the equal sign.

Enclosing the entire vale with double quotes is mandatory when you have situations where the value you are assigning to variable name has white spaces or dot

varname="This is a beautiful day and it is 8:00am "

How to display the values of variables

All variables are assigned values in a intention to use them in various ways in the program. To access the value of variable which is assigned a value, prefix the variable name with "$" sign.

varname=100

echo $varname

Note if you try to display the value of a variable name, for which the value has never been assigned, it prints blank (null)

Apart from defining and assigning values to variables within the scripts/programs, there are several variables which are automatically set whenever you login such as HOME, MAIL, PATH, PS1 EDITOR etc. All variables defined in any users environment is available for that user to use in any programs he or she runs.

For Loop

Flow of control is part and parcel of any programming language. Shell also provides several flow control features and one of the most popular one is "For loop"

One of the program control feature in shell programming is branching and looping.

Looping is a special feature where a portion of a program is repeated until it reaches a certain criteria.or condition

The for loop is almost universally held to be the most commonly used loop. This is extremely useful when you have to execute a given set of instruction, limited number of times with little or no changes.

This loop will start with giving a variable a predefined value and then keep on executing the body part of the loop as long as the given condition is true. Every time the loop is executed, the variable gets a new value.

Whenever you like a section of code to be repeated a fixed number of times During each iteration, a special variable called a loop variable is set to a different value based on the range specified.

The syntax for the **for loop** construct

for variable [in list]
do
    command
    command
    command
    ....
done

variable is any shell variable , the number of items specified in list determines the number of times the commands enclosed within do and done would be executed.

command represents any shell command or command line.

The reserved words **do** and **done** must be preceded by a newline or ; (semicolon).

while and until statements

Both these constructs allow a section of code to be run repetitively while a certain condition holds true.

while construct, unlike the for:in:do construct, checks the TRUE or FALSE value of a condition before proceeding.

The syntax for **while** construct is:

while condition
do
  command
  command
done

For until construct syntax, just substitute **until** for **while** in the above example.

Only difference between **while** and **until** is the way the condition is handled. In while, the loop executes as long as the condition is true; in **until**, it runs as long as the condition is false. But the until condition is checked at the top of the loop, not at the bottom.

until construct which is very similar to the while loop construct. The construct works in precisely the same manner with one exception that it repeats a series of commands until a condition is met.

The result is that you can convert any **until** into a **while** by simply negating the condition. The only place where **until** might be better is something like this:

until condition;
 do
   command
   command
done

The case statements

Case is yet an another flow control construct that facilitates for multi-way branching based on patterns. Case statement is handy when you wish to compare a value against a whole series of values. The same result can be achieved by using if-elif statement chain, however case statement is more concise and easy to read and write.

This construct lets you express a series of if-then-else type statements in a concise way.

The syntax of case is as follows:

case expression in
  pattern1)
      command statements ; ;
  pattern2)

command statements ; ;

....

esac

In above example the expression is compared with each *pattern* until a match is found, at which point the associated *command statements* are executed

When all the command statements are executed for a given pattern match, control is passed to the first statement after the esac. Each list of commands must end with a double semi-colon (;;).

The patterns are evaluated in the order in which they are seen, and only the first pattern that matches will be executed. Often, you may want to include a ``none of the above'' clause; to do this, use * as your last pattern.

For example

case "$x"
in
   0)   echo "The value of x is zero" ;;
   1)   echo "The value of x is one" ;;
   2)   echo "The value of x is two" ;;
   3)   echo "The value of x is three" ;;
   *)   echo "Invalid value" ;;
esac

if statement

In any programming language, variables are one of the main components where they are used as placeholders. Testing the condition of variable is quite important. The if statement is some kind of conditional statement, which allows you to test the condition of variable and also execute set of instructions based on the outcome of condition testing.

In if statement you use a condition when you want to choose whether or not to do something, or to choose among a small number of things to do according to the truth or falsehood of conditions.

The **if** construct has the following syntax:

if condition
then
   statements   **(if condition is true)**
[elif condition   **(if condition is true)**
   then statements….]
[else
   statements] **(if condition is false)**
fi

Adding else clause gives you the ability to execute another set of statements if a condition is false. elsif clause gives you the ability to have multiple if statements in one if statement. **if** construct supports as many **elif** clauses as you wish.

Exit command and status

Shell script normally consists of series of commands, and gets executed as per the flow within the script. What if you would like to exit out of the script before it's completion for whatever reason. You may also wish to exit out of the script whenever a command within the script encounters errors.

The **exit** command can be used to terminate a script. exit command returns a value, which is available to the script's parent process.

All shell commands returns an exit status. This exit status helps to determine the successful or unsuccessful status of the command. This exist status is sometime referred as return status. When the command runs successfully it returns an exit state equals to zero. Similarly when the command runs unsuccessfully, which in shell terminology interpreted as an error code, returns a non-zero value.

When a shell script is run, the last command execution status determines the execution status of the script itself. If the last command runs successfully, the exit status of the script is treated as successful. If the last command runs unsuccessfully, the exit status of the script is treated as unsuccessful. The similar terminology applies to functions as well.

Often **exit *nnn*** command is used within the shell scripts, to deliver an nnn exit status to the parent shell.

Shell scripts and functions returns an integer code to its calling process. This is called the exit status. 0 is usually the "OK" exit status,

The exit status of any command can be explained well using if statement.

For example

If the status is 0, the condition evaluates to true;

if command ran successfully
then
     normal processing
else
     error processing
fi

Combinations of Exit Statuses

Usually flow-control operators involve making some conditional test and branching on the result (true/false).

The && Operator

&& operator is used to execute a command and, if it is successful, execute the next command in the list.

For example:

cmd1 && cmd2

In above example *cmd1 is* executed and its exit status is examined. cmd2 execution depends on the cmd1 execution status. cmd2 executes, only if *cmd1* succeeds. In other words the logic works similar to following if/then statement

```
if cmd1
then
  cmd2
fi
```

For example

If you have two statements like "statement1 && statement2", this means execute statement1, and if its exit status is 0, execute statement2
The statements like "statement1 || statement2" means execute statement1 and regardless of it's exit statement is 0 or not, execute statement2

```
if statement1 && statement2
then
    .....
fi
```

The || operator

|| operator is used to execute a command and, if it fails, execute the next command in the command list. For example:

cmd1 || cmd2

if statement1 || statement2
then
     ....
fi

If statement1 succeeds, then statement2 does not run. This makes statement1 the last statement, which means that the **then** clause runs. On the other hand, if statement1 fails, then statement2 runs, and if statement2 runs successfully only then the commands after **then** statement are executed.

Operators used in shell

Throughout the shell programming, you normally use quite a number of relational operators. Some used as arithmetic test operators; some used as string comparison operators and some as file attribute operators

Arithmetic Operators

Operator	Description	Used to test if
-eq	equal to	two integers are equal
-ne	not equal to	two integers are not equal
-le	less than or equal	one integer is less than or equal to another
-lt	less than	one integer is less than another

-ge	greater than or equal to	one integer is greater than or equal to
-gt	greater than	one integer greater than another
-z	zero length	a string has zero length
-n	non zero length	a string has non zero length
=	string comparison for equality	two strings are equal
! =	unequal comparison for strings	two strings are not equal
-a file	Check file	true if file exists
-d file	Check file is a directory	true if file is a directory

Break and continue statements

One more interesting statement while dealing with iteration and looping is break and continue statement.

To terminate innermost enclosing loop use single "break" command. This will cause the innermost loop execution to terminate and resume after the nearest done statement.

The syntax is

break

Suppose you multiple nested loops and you wish to exit out of predetermined number of nesting, use

break n

This command will exit from *n* levels and resume the execution to resume after the done n levels up.

continue statement

There could be situations where one of the iteration in a given loops reports errors, but you wish to continue with the rest of the iteration and execution. There is a command in shell which is handy to use situations like this.

The only difference between break and continue command is, in case of continue command, it causes the current iteration of the loop to exit, rather than the entire loop.

The syntax is

continue

Just like break statement you could use arguments with **continue** command

continue n

Special variable

Apart from the user-defined variables and environment variables, there are other built-in variables that are vital to shell programming.

As we already aware variables play very important role in shell programming. To make the shell programming more effective shell has some special variables which can be used in any shell script or program.

Positional Parameters

Position variables are passed to the scripts in the form of parameters, that is why it would be more appropriate to call them as positional parameters. The positional parameters are passed to programs/scripts in the form of parameters in command line

For example

./script.sh   servername   database_name

In above example you are trying to run a script called **"script.sh"** and passing two parameters called **"servername"** and **"database_name"**

When script starts executing the shell, it assigns internally these two parameters as $1 and $2

$1= **$servername**

$2= **$database_name**

Within the script the value of two parameters "servername" and "database_name"

can be addressed using $1 and $2

Positional parameters are always numbered and are referred to with a proceeding ``$": **$1, $2, $3**, and so on.

There are nine positional parameters. Named as **[$1 -$9]**

The shell allows a command line to contain at least 128 arguments; however, a shell program is restricted to referencing only nine positional parameters, **$1** through **$9**, at a given time. You can work around this restriction by using the **shift** command.

Shell has more special variables like positional parameters

For example:

If you have a shell script with name script.sh and positional parameters such as hostname and oracle_sid,

./script.sh   servername   database_name

servername   and   database_name would be positional variables 1 and 2 respectively and script.sh would be the positional variable 0.

$0 ->This is another special variable which represents the name of the command currently being executed.

$# ->This special variable represents number of positional parameters passed in the above   script (script.sh). Since we passed two positional parameters, so the value of $# would be 2

$* ->This special variable represents all positional parameters in sequence

$? ->This special variable represents the exit status of the last command executed. When the last command executed successfully, it returns the exit status as 0(zero), if unsuccessful it returns non-zero exit status.

$! ->This special variable represents the process id of the last command run in the background.

$$ ->This special variable represents process number of this shell.

Arithmetic Operators

Though shell does not provide any built-in mechanisms to enable you to perform arithmetic operation on shell variables, shell does comes with the program   called expr that is used to evaluate expressions in shell programming.

By default **expr** program writes it's output to standard output. However by using back-quote mechanism, you can assign expr's result to a shell variable.

For example

$sum=`expr  10 + 23`
$echo $sum
33
$

Read data from terminal

Within the shell program there may be situations, where you need to enter data from the terminal. On unix there is command called **"read"** which can read data from the terminal.

For example

read x y z

When you execute the above command the shell reads a line from the terminal and assign the values to the shell variables. We have three variables x, y and z . Values typed are delimited by blanks or tabs.

Part 5

Chapter 10

File Manipulation on Unix

Unix has many powerful utilities to process the content of a file

grep command

grep command is one of the patterns matching command. This command searches each line in a given file for the given word or string. This command searches a file globally for lines matching a given regular expression, and prints them.

grep command searches a text file for a string or for a regular expression. Regular expressions are formed by combining the ordinary characters with one or more meta characters

You can search multiple files for a given pattern. Meta characters can be specified for filenames as well as pattern search within the file.

grep command has may options, however some of the most handy ones are

options

-i   Ignores upper/lower case distinction with the pattern

-n   Precedes each line by its line number in the file (first line is 1) for the match.

-v   Prints all lines except those that contain the pattern.

-c   Prints only a count of the lines that contain the pattern.

For example:-

1. Ignores upper/lower case

$cat datafile.lst|grep -i "DOC"

/data/oradata/PROD1/doc_data_01.dbf
/data/oradata/PROD1/doc_indx01.dbf

2. Precedes each line by its line number

Scat datafile.lst|grep -n "doc"

5:/data/oradata/PROD1/doc_data_01.dbf
6:/data/oradata/PROD1/doc_indx01.dbf

3. Prints all lines except those with pattern
$cat datafile.lst|grep -v "doc"
/data/oradata/PROD1/tools01.dbf
/data/oradata/PROD1/sysaux01.dbf
/data/oradata/PROD1/undo01.dbf
/data/oradata/PROD1/system01.dbf
/data/oradata/PROD1/test_data01.dbf
/data/oradata/PROD1/test_indx01.dbf

4. Prints only a count of the lines with the match

Scat datafile.lst|grep -c "doc"

2

Sort command

Sort command is another file processing utility on Unix. It is basically a database tool. Individual fields can be sorted on and it allows you to specify the type of sort to be carried out on it.

Unless you tell it otherwise, sort divides each line into fields at white space (blanks or tabs), and sorts the lines by field from left to right.

In general the lines in a file are sorted in the following order.

Firstly the lines starting with numbers, then lines starting with upper-case letters, this is followed by lines starting with lower-case letters and finally symbols such as % and !

By default sort command sorts always from left to right, however you can start the sort from any field number by using option +n and –n is used to stop sorting on filed n. Please note that the sort counts fields from left to right and starts with 0 (zero).

The general syntax

Sort filename

To sort a file on filed 4 use the command

Specific field Sort

During sort each line in a file is treated as series of fields, separated by a delimiter. By default the delimiter between the field is space. However this default delimiter character can be changed .

For example

To specify the delimiter character as (:) colon use –t option with the delimiter character

Sort +3 –4 filename

+3 indicates sort on 4th field of each line (first field is indicated by 0), -4 indicates to stop sorting at the end of filed 4 (beginning of fifth field).

Numeric sort

Fields are separated by white space, however you can use the -t option to separate by any character. The -n options tells sort to sort a numeric key, otherwise it will sort by the corresponding ASCII values.

Sort hints

sort -u sorts the file and eliminates duplicate lines

If you want to sort on a field basis

sort –uk1,1   filename   which would sort first on line and then sorts on first filed

Sort –uk2,2 filename

This sorts on field 2

Note 1:- If there are any duplicate rows in the file, they get eliminated and only one row is reported

Note 2: One more important option is -b; this tells sort to ignore extra white space at the beginning of each field

Case-Insensitive Sorts

If you don't care about the difference between uppercase and lowercase letters, invoke sort with the -f (case-fold) option. This folds lowercase letters into uppercase. In other words, it treats all letters as uppercase

Reverse Sort

The -r option tells sort to "reverse" the order of the sort

Cut Command

cut command "cuts out" (extracts) columns from a table or fields from each line in a file. Fields may be specified by numerical position or in terms of character offset. By default, fields are taken to be separated by white space.

cut command cut's out selected fields of each line of a file. use the cut utility to cut out columns from a table or fields from each line of a file;

The basic format of the cut command is

cut -clist files

For example

-c option specifies that cut would be done on specific character
list specifies which character position to cut.

Options are interpreted as follows:

list

A comma-separated list of integer *byte* (-b option), *character* (-c option), or *field* (-f option) numbers, in increasing order, with optional - to indicate ranges. For example:

1,4,7

Positions 1, 4, and 7.

1-3,8

Positions 1 through 3 and 8.

-5,10

Positions 1 through 5 and 10.

3-

Position 3 through last position.

-b *list*

> Cut based on a list of bytes. Each selected byte is output unless the -n option is also specified.

-c *list*

> Cut based on character positions specified by *list* (-c 1-72 extracts the first 72 characters of each line).

-f *list*

> Where *list* is a list of fields assumed to be separated in the file by a delimiter character (see -d); for example, -f 1,7 copies the first and seventh field only. Lines with no field delimiters will be passed through intact (useful for table subheadings), unless -s is specified.

-d *char*

> The character following -d is the field delimiter (-f option only). Default is *tab*. Space or other characters with special meaning to the shell must be quoted. Adjacent field delimiters delimit null fields. *char* may be an international code set character.

-n

> Do not split characters. If the high end of a range within a list is not the last byte of a character, that character is not included in the output. However, if the low end of a range within a list is not the first byte of a character, the entire character *is* included in the output."

-s

> Suppresses lines with no delimiter characters when using -f option. Unless -s is specified, lines with no delimiters appear in the output without alteration.

For example:-

cut –c1 phonebook

In above example first character of each line in the file "phonebook" would be cut.

You can selectively cut more than one character from each line, by listing character positions to be cut, separated by commas.

For example

cut -1, 7 phonebook

In above example first through seventh character from each line of the file "phonebook" would be cut

Password file mapping of user ID to user names:
cut -d : -f 1,5 /etc/passwd

awk utility

Awk is a pattern matching and processing language. It searches input for patterns and performs actions on each line of input that satisfies the pattern. awk is also considered as a programming language and it is pre-dominently designed for processing text-based data.

The **awk** command utilizes a set of user-supplied instructions to compare a set of files, one line at a time, to extended regular expressions supplied by the user. Then actions are performed upon any line that matches the extended regular expressions.

The **awk** command takes two types of inputs. input text files and program instructions. awk executes a set of instructions for each line of input. You can specify instructions on the command line or create a script file.

For command lines, the syntax is:

awk 'instructions' files

Input is read one line at a time from one or more files or from standard input. The instructions must be enclosed in single quotes to protect them from the shell. (Instructions almost always contain curly braces and/or dollar signs, which are interpreted as special characters by the shell). Multiple command lines can be entered separating commands with semicolons or using the multi line input capability of the Bourne shell.

Awk programs are usually placed in a file where they can be tested and modified. The syntax for invoking awk with a script file is:

awk -f script files

Awk, in the usual case, interprets each input line as a record and each word on that line, delimited by spaces or tabs, as a field. (These defaults can be changed.) One or more consecutive spaces or tabs count as a single delimiter.

$0 represents the entire input line. $1, $2, ... refer to the individual fields on the input line.

For Example:-

$ awk '{ print $1 }' list
John
Alice
Orville
Terry

In the next example, a pattern "/MA/" is specified. The default action is to print each line that matches the pattern.

$ awk '/MA/' list
James Daggett, 341 King Road, Plymouth MA
Serra Evans, 20 Post Road, Sudbury MA
Sal Carpenter, 73 6th Street, Boston MA

The next example uses a print statement to limit the output to the first field of each record.

$ awk '/MA/ { print $1 }' list
James
Serra
Sal

In the next example, we use the -F option to change the field separator to a comma. This allows us to retrieve any of three fields: the full name, the street address, or the city and state.

$ awk -F, '/MA/ { print $1 }' list
James Daggett
Serra Adams
Sal Carpenter

In the next example, we print each field on its own line. Multiple commands are separated by semicolons.

$ awk -F, '{ print $1; print $2; print $3 }' list
James Daggett
341 King Road
Plymouth MA

Substitute data
If you want to **Substitute data in between the fields**

$awk '{print $1"."$2}' list

James.Daggett,
Serra.Evans
Sal.Carpenter

$awk '{print $1 " This is the border line " $2}' list

James **This is the border line** Daggett,
Serra **This is the border line** Evans
Sal **This is the border line** Carpenter

File processing using AWK

Example:-

For example if you have a database with over 100 data files and you want to migrate this database to a different storage device. Your task is to prepare the move and also the rollback scripts if change/move needed to be rolled back

For example:-
The list of files to be relocated are in

$cat datafile.lst

```
/data/oradata/PROD1/tools01.dbf
/data/oradata/PROD1/sysaux01.dbf
/data/oradata/PROD1/undo01.dbf
/data/oradata/PROD1/system01.dbf
/data/oradata/PROD1/doc_data_01.dbf
/data/oradata/PROD1/doc_indx01.dbf
/data/oradata/PROD1/test_data01.dbf
/data/oradata/PROD1/test_indx01.dbf
```

The command to process the file would be as follows and the output from the command would be written to cp_datafiles.sh

$cat   datafile.lst |awk   -F/   '{print   "cp   " $0   " /newlocation/"$2"/"$3"/"$4"/"$5}' > cp_datafiles.sh

$cat cp_datafiles.sh

```
cp                                /data/oradata/PROD1/tools01.dbf
/newlocation/data/oradata/PROD1/tools01.dbf
cp                                /data/oradata/PROD1/sysaux01.dbf
/newlocation/data/oradata/PROD1/sysaux01.dbf
cp                                /data/oradata/PROD1/undo01.dbf
/newlocation/data/oradata/PROD1/undo01.dbf
cp                                /data/oradata/PROD1/system01.dbf
/newlocation/data/oradata/PROD1/system01.dbf
cp                               /data/oradata/PROD1/doc_data_01.dbf
/newlocation/data/oradata/PROD1/doc_data_01.dbf
cp                               /data/oradata/PROD1/doc_indx01.dbf
/newlocation/data/oradata/PROD1/doc_indx01.dbf
```

```
cp                                    /data/oradata/PROD1/test_data01.dbf
/newlocation/data/oradata/PROD1/test_data01.dbf
cp                                    /data/oradata/PROD1/test_indx01.dbf
/newlocation/data/oradata/PROD1/test_indx01.dbf
```

$0   →Represents the entire line
-F/   →Represents the field separator is /

Rollback script to move the files back to it's original location

The following command maps files back to it's original location where it was originally residing (Rollback)

$cat cp_datafiles.sh|awk '{print $1" "$3" "$2}'

```
cp                          /newlocation/data/oradata/PROD1/tools01.dbf
/data/oradata/PROD1/tools01.dbf
cp                          /newlocation/data/oradata/PROD1/sysaux01.dbf
/data/oradata/PROD1/sysaux01.dbf
cp                          /newlocation/data/oradata/PROD1/undo01.dbf
/data/oradata/PROD1/undo01.dbf
cp                          /newlocation/data/oradata/PROD1/system01.dbf
/data/oradata/PROD1/system01.dbf
cp                          /newlocation/data/oradata/PROD1/doc_data_01.dbf
/data/oradata/PROD1/doc_data_01.dbf
cp                          /newlocation/data/oradata/PROD1/doc_indx01.dbf
/data/oradata/PROD1/doc_indx01.dbf
cp                          /newlocation/data/oradata/PROD1/test_data01.dbf
/data/oradata/PROD1/test_data01.dbf
cp                          /newlocation/data/oradata/PROD1/test_indx01.dbf
/data/oradata/PROD1/test_indx01.dbf
```

File usage (fuser)

Description

The fuser utility displays the process IDs of the processes that are using the files specified as arguments.

Usage:- Useful when you notice that a given file is held up with another stubborn process and you want to identify this process and release the file. Handy while rolling back failed patch

1. **fuser filename** → Indicates that the process is using the file

For Example:-

$fuser system01.dbf

system01.dbf: **22700**o   22624o   22618o   22616o   22614o   22612o   22609o   22604o   22600o

$ps -ef|grep **22700**

   oracle 18887 18860   0 13:30:46 pts/23   0:00 grep 22700
   oracle **22700** 13823   0   Jul 25 ?   184:22 ora_mmnl_RMNTEST

2. **fuser –u system01.dbf** → Indicates that the process is using the file along with userid who owns these processes

system01.dbf: 22700o(oracle)   22624o(oracle)   22618o(oracle)   22616o(oracle)   22614o(oracle)   22612o(oracle)   22609o(oracle)   22604o(oracle)   22600o(oracle)

3. **fuser –uk filename.dbf** →Releases the file from associated processes (Kills the processes)

Note:- If the **fuser –u** command doesn't return a userid connected to the file, run **fuser –c** command to identify the processes associated with file

XARGS Utility - Construct argument lists and invoke utility

Description:-

The xargs utility constructs a command line consisting of the utility and argument operands specified followed by as many arguments read in sequence from standard input.

The xargs utility then invokes the constructed command line and waits for its completion. This sequence is repeated until an end-of-file condition is detected on standard input

For example : If you want to list out all the files which has the word "UPGRADE" in it under oracle home directory and list all these files in /tmp/upgrade.log

You could try this command

cd $ORACLE_HOME/bin

ls –ltr|xargs grep UPGRADE >/tmp/upgrade.log

In following example, content from the first file is been processed using cut command before been passed to xargs command.

cat tmp.log|cut -f1 -d":"|xargs ls -ltr >backup_logs.lst
cat test.sql|grep "'"|cut -f2 -d"'"|xargs -n1 ls -la

Locate files that contain certain strings

Sometimes you may have to locate files that contain certain strings and this can be done by using **find** and **grep** commands to search for a file containing a specific string.

In the following example, unix will search your current directory and all subdirectories, looking in all files for the text "v$session".

>find . –print|xargs grep -i v\$session

find:- Generates a list of all files in the current directory and in all directories underneath the current directory.

-print : Causes the find command to actually display the list of files. This display is piped into xargs.

xargs : Performs the grep command for each file displayed by the find command.

grep –i v\\$session :- Filters out all lines except those that contain "v$session".

Chapter 11
All about Text editing in Unix

vi editor

vi is a family of screen-oriented test editor. On unix text editors are used to edit text files. Technically text editor is a type of program.

In previous chapters we have discussed about the command – line editing and command-line editing is enabled using any standard editor.

You can enable command-line editing either by setting editing mode using environment variable VISUAL or by selecting an editing mode by setting the option explicitly with the set –o command.

To set emacs editor

$set –o emacs

or

To set vi editor

$set –o vi

When you start writing programs in shell, it is very handy to use vi editor, though vi editor has various features, once you understand the essentials it is easy to play around vi editor

vi editor is a screen-based editor and majority of unix users do use vi editors.

Since vi editors use full screen, it is important you set the TERM variable to the appropriate terminal type. For example vt100, hp etc.

To set your vt100 as your terminal type

On C Shell (/bin/csh)

set term=vt100

On Korn shell(/bin/ksh) or Bourne shell (/bin/sh)

TERM=vt100
export TERM

Once you have your TERM variable set, you can start the vi editor. You can edit new files or existing files using vi editor.

To create new file or edit existing file, just enter vi followed by filename (temp)

For example

vi temp

when you hit enter, it opens a screen full of tildes (~) on left side of the screen. At the bottom of the screen you see the name of the file as follows when "temp" is a new file

~

~

~

~

"temp" [New file]

If temp is an existing file it would display the name of the file, number of lines and the number of characters in the file as follows

This is line number 1

This is line number 2

~

~

~

~

"temp" 2 lines, 44 characters

vi modes

When you open the vi editor you are automatically placed in *command* mode, In this mode you would be allowed to enter short commands. However this mode would not allow you to enter any text.

vi has another mode called *insert* mode. In this mode you would be able to enter text within the editor. You can get into insert mode by entering key **a** or **i** on your key board. You can get out of insert mode by hitting the **escape** key which would place you in **command** mode.

There are number commands available to enter when you are in command mode. Some of the most commonly used handy ones are as follows

vi commands in command mode

Command	Description
a	Enter into *insert* mode from *command* mode
i	Enter into *insert* mode from *command* mode
h	Move the cursor to left one position.
j	Move cursor down one line
l	Move the cursor right one character
w	Move the cursor right one word
b	Move the cursor left one word
e	Move to end of current word
r	Replace one character under the cursor
0	Move to beginning of line
^	Move to first non-blank character in line
$	Move to end of line

Note:- All of these commands except the last three can be preceded by a number that acts as a repeat

Yanking and cutting

Another important feature of vi command mode command is yanking and cutting. This is used to delete the content within the vi editor selectively. The general command used for cutting is **d**

When you are in command mode, entering **dd** would delete the current line. If you wish to delete multiple lines from current line, just precede the dd command with number of lines.

For example **5dd** would delete 5 lines from current line.

Some handy yanking and cutting commands are as follows

5dd deletes five lines from current cursor position downwards
d$ deletes from current cursor position to the end of the line.
d^   deletes from current cursor position to the beginning of the line.

dw   deletes from current cursor position to the end of the word.

Yanking and Pasting

Similar to cutting, there are commands available for selecting lines and pasting within vi editor. To yank the text use *yy* preceded by number of lines and to past the selected number of lines use *p*

For example

To select 5 lines and past it with vi editor

Move the cursor to the first line in command mode, enter **5yy**, when you are still in command mode which would yank 5 lines below your cursor, move your cursor to the location where you wish to paste these lines and enter **p**

un-delete command

What if you have done a mistake while typing inside the vi editor and you would like to undo the last text modification. The command **u** undoes the last text modification command
u undoes only the last modification command. While **U** undoes all such commands on the current line.

Handy commands while using vi editor

You might find following commands handy while working with vi Editor.

1. Write to a New File

You can use **:w** to save an entire buffer (the copy of the file you are editing) under a new filename

:w new_file1

2. Saving part of the file (1 to 20 lines of the file to new file newfile2

:1, 20 w newfile2

3. From line 230 to end of the file would be saved to newfile3

:230,$ w newfile3

4. From current line to line 600 is saved to newfile4

:.,600 w newfile4   →Note the dot which indicates current

5. Substitute

First character on 1 to 10 lines would be replaced by word **"create user"** .
:1,10s/^/create user /

6. To append to existing file

You can use the UNIX redirect and append operator (>>) with **w** to append all or part of the contents of the buffer to an existing file. For example, if you entered:

:1,10w newfile

and then:

:340,$w >>newfile

newfile would contain lines 1-10 and line 340 to the end of the buffer.

7. To insert a character or Change the word
i
   insert
cw
   change word

8. Wipe out all changes

What if you want to wipe out all of the edits you have made in a session and then return to the original file? The command:

:e! [RETURN]

returns you to the last saved version of the file, so you can start over.

9. Saving into existing file:

Type **:w!** file to overwrite the existing file, or type **:w** newfile to save the edited version in a new file.

Insert text	i any text you like
Return to command mode	[ESC]
Quit vi, saving edits	ZZ

10. Single Movements within command mode in vi editor

The keys h, j, k, and l, right under your fingertips, will move the cursor:

h

  left, one space.

j

  down, one line.

k

  up, one line.

l

  right, one space.

Sed editor

Sed is an stream editor. It is a powerful utility if used well. This stream editor is predominantly used on a command line as well as in unix shell programs. sed has several commands. Among all most popular one is substitute command. We will only cover the essential handy commands in this chapter, and full detail on all commands on sed would be beyond the scope of this book.

Substitute command

Substitute command is popularly used to change all occurrences of the regular expressions into a new value.

For example

sed s/dark/light/ <old_file>new_file

In above example *s* stands for the substitute. All regular patterns of word "**dark**" are replaced by word "**light**" in the file "**old_file**" and written to newly create file "**new_file**"

If you like to escape any special character use slash as a delimiter (\)

For example

sed 's/\/common\/bin/\/temp\/bin/' <old_file>new_file

There are number of utilities available on unix that work on files. On almost all utilities by default it would change only the first occurrence of the word on a line. What if you want to make the change on every word on the line instead of the first. Sed has a special flag to address this issue and it is called global replacement

Global replacement (/g)

If you have multiple occurrence (more than one occurrence of pattern) on a single line
For example

sed 's/dark/light/g' <old_file>new_file

In above example all multiple occurrences of word "**dark**" is replaced globally by word **"light"** in every line of the file "**old_file**" and new file is written to "**new_file**"

Part 6

Chapter 12

Transfer files and directories between unix system

Introduction

Unix servers normally configured in a networked environment. Often there is a necessity exists to transfer files between two unix servers within the network.

rcp command is one of the popular command to transfer files from local hosts to remote hosts. The syntax of the rcp command is as follows

rcp host_name:file_name host_name:file_name

To make the above command work you need to have an account on the unix host you want to copy the files to and from. Secondly you need to have a special file called .rhosts in your login directory on the other unix host

.rhosts file acts as an authentication file, that allows anyone to copy files between the hosts. Each line in the .rhosts file has the name of the remote host and also the username on that host.

In above example it is assumed that you have an account on the remote host just like the account on local host.

However you can still transfer files between two remote hosts with different account details. All you need to do is address the account detail in the command line.

For example

rcp **host_name:filename username@host_name:filename**

ftp program

Chapter 12: Transfer files and directories between unix
system

Files also can be transferred between remote hosts using
another popular program called ftp. ftp is the acronym for file
transfer protocol.

To start using ftp program, simply type ftp at your command
prompt and this will return the ftp prompt (ftp>)

ftp

ftp>

Once you are greeted with this ftp prompt you are ready to
enter ftp commands. ftp program has number of commands
and whole list of commands can be available by typing
question mark (?) at the ftp prompt.

ftp> ?
Commands may be abbreviated. Commands are:

!	cr	mdir	protect	safe
$	delete	mechanism	proxy	send
account	debug	mget	put	sendport
append	dir	mkdir	pwd	site
ascii	disconnect	mls	quit	status
bell	form	mode	quote	struct
binary	get	mput	recv	sunique
bye	glob	nlist	reget	tcpwindow
case	hash	nmap	remotehelp	tenex
ccc	help	ntrans	rename	trace
cd	lcd	open	reset	type
cdup	ls	passive	restart	user
clear	macdef	private	rmdir	verbose
close	mdelete	prompt	runique	?

ftp>

To get a description on individual commands use the help as follows

ftp> help mget
mget   get multiple files

When you use the ftp program, the commands are similar irrespective of whether you use them locally or remotely. When you work on remote server you need to open the connection to make your commands work.

Open remote host connection

From the ftp program if you wish to open a connection to remote host use the command "open hostname"

ftp>open hostname

The above command would prompt you to enter the authentication details. Enter valid username and password on the remote host.

Once you are through the authentication you would be placed in the home directory of this userid. You can create, change directories etc once you are within this remote host.

To make directory

ftp>mkdir scripts

To change the directory

ftp>cd scripts

To list the files on remote directory

Chapter 12: Transfer files and directories between unix
system

ftp>ls

To send a single file from your current directory on the local
host to the current directory on the remote host you could use
send or put command. They work the same way

   ftp>send file_name
   ftp>put file_name

To send multiple files from your current directory on the
local host to the current directory on the remote host, use
"mput" command.

ftp>mput *.*

Above command transfers all files from current directory on
local host to the current directory on the remote host.
However before transferring each file it would prompt you to
confirm.

To avoid prompting at every file transfer you could type
command "prompt" and this will transfer all files without
prompting for your confirmation.

ftp>prompt
ftp>mput *.*

Just like transferring the files from local host to the remote
host, you could transfer files from remote host to your local
host. This can be done my using "**get**" and "**mget**" commands
for single file and multiple file transfer.

To send a single file from your current directory on the remote host to the current directory on the local host you could use get command.

ftp>get file_name

To send multiple files from your current directory on the remote host to the current directory on the local host, use "mget" command.

ftp>prompt
ftp>mget *.*

Though rcp and ftp are widely used programs to transfer files across the hosts in the network, when it comes to security, they may not be considered to be safe.

Unix has an another secured program called **"scp"** acronym for secured copy

scp for secured file copy

scp commands are widely used these days, because of the security concerns. You can transfer files as well as directories between remote hosts without starting ftp session. Scp does uses a password and passphrase for authentication. The main difference between scp and ftp are, scp encrypts both the file and any passwords exchanged over the metwork, which makes scp safer than ftp.

The syntax for scp would look like this

scp scripts.sh oracle@hostname:/home/oracle

The above command would transfer the file "script.sh" from local servers current directory to /home/oracle directory on servername called "hostname" using the account "oracle"

ssh program

These days security has become a main concern, when you operate within the network, There is a possibility that you often need to communicate among the untrusted network hosts, having said that rcp and rlogin programs are loosing the momentum and we have a more trusted program called ssh. ssh provides secure encrypted communication between two untrusted hosts over an insecure network.

Intention of ssh is to replace rsh and rlogin. ssh is widely used to logging into a remote machine and for executing commands on a remote machine. It provides equivalent functionality as rlogin utility except that ssh is more secure.

ssh connections are authenticated using "passphrase" authentication. Authentication setup needs to be done only once by generating private/public key pair.

How to setup passphrase authentication

- Check ssh is installed on your local machine
- Check you have directory $HOME/.ssh on your local machine
- Run ssh-keygen -t rsa OR ssh-keygen -t dsa command which will create two files id_rsa OR id_dsa in your $HOME/.ssh directory.
- id_rsa OR id_dsa file is the private key and it also generates public key files called id_rsa.pub OR id_dsa.pub

- During the run, you will be prompted to enter "passphrase", text similar to password

Once you generate private and public keys, you need to copy the public keys to the remote server where you wish to access

- On the remote machine make a directory $HOME/.ssh
- Copy the content of $HOME/.ssh/id_rsa.pub OR id_dsa.pub file on your local machine to a file called $HOME/.ssh/authorized_keys2 on your remote server.
- Logout from remote server and try to connect from local server using ssh and it should authenticate you with "passphrase"

Chapter 13

Unix File System and Disk Management

Compared to modern days the computer disks were smaller in olden days. To make the bigger disk, the several physical disks were logically grouped to make a single larger disk. This group of physical disks were called virtual disk. This type of arrangement helped to create larger filesystems.

In recent time disk has become relatively affordable, and available in larger sizes. So instead of making one virtual disk out of number of physical disks, number of virtual diska are created out of one physical disk. These virtual disk are called disk partitions.

Disks exist in Unix as physical volumes and are carved into physical partitions. These physical partitions are in turn, assigned to logical volumes. A logical volume is a chunk of storage that consists of one or more physical partitions. The logical volumes are then mapped onto Unix mount points. Several logical volumes can be used in a mount point, and a collection of such logical volumes is referred to as a volume group. A unix mount point is like a directory name, and is used by you, the Oracle DBA, when allocating Oracle data files.

Logical Volume Management (LVM)

LVM is simply an additional abstraction layer between the physical storage medium and your data that makes system design and administrative changes easier once the file system is in use.

What is Logical Volume Management..?

The foundation of Logical Volume Management is the "Physical Volume". Physical volumes match up 1-to-1 with existing disk-level partitions. Just like "traditional" partitions a physical disk can have multiple physical volumes but physical volumes cannot exceed the maximum size of the disk they occupy. Unlike a traditional partition a Physical Volume is not formatted with a file system, it is just there to support a Volume Group.

Volume Groups are composed of one or more Physical Volumes. Even if you have only one disk and create only one disk-level partition resulting in a single Physical Volume you still must create a Volume Group composed of that single volume. Physical Volumes can be added to and removed from Volume Groups but Volume Groups cannot be resized arbitrarily, they are the sum of their underlying Physical Volumes. It is with Volume Groups that you get your first real layer of abstraction from the physical disk, you can have multiple Volume Groups on a single physical disk or multiple physical disks in a single Volume Group.

Logical Volumes are the functional equivalent of disk-level partitions, they are where the file system and your data reside. Logical Volumes are created within Volume Groups similar to the way that traditional partitions are created on physical disks. There is nothing to say that a Logical Volume can't consume an entire Volume Group, and Logical Volumes from multiple Volume Groups can be joined in a single directory structure but a single Logical Volume cannot span multiple Volume Groups.

List logical Volumes in HP-UX

All logical volumes can be listed in HP-UX using the df –k command. The df –k command shows each logical volume and the corresponding mount point.
For example:

>df –k
The df –k command is most often used to see the total space in each mount point and the amount of free space within each mount point.

To see the logical volumes in a file system, you can issue the lvdisplay command followed by a logical volume   name . For example

>lvdisplay /dev/vg00/u01

The following lsvg –o command can be used to display a list of volume groups with Unix mounts

>lsvg -o

Now that you can see the volume groups, you can drill-in using lsvg –l to see details for a specific volume group.

>lsvg –l appvg01

You can even get fancy and use the xargs command to display the details for all volume groups in the list. For example:

>lsvg -o|xargs –lsvg –l

Display Unix Mount Points

A mount point is a Unix location of disk storage. There are two main commands to display logical volumes and mount points: bdf and df

Display Mount Points in HP-UX

The bdf command is used in HP-UX, to display the logical volumes and mount points for each filesystem. For example

>bdf

Display mount points in AIX and Solaris

In AIX and Solaris, the df command is used to display mount points. For example

>df –k

Show Mount Points for a Physical Disk in AIX

To be effective, you as the Oracle DBA, should know the mapping between physical disks, logical volumes, and mount points. Without this information, it is very difficult to find an I/O problem. In an earlier section, you saw how to use the iostat command to find physical disks that have excessive I/O. To map a physical disk to logical volumes and mount points, you can use the lspv commands.

>lspv –l hdisk7

Here, you can see that the physical disk bdisk7 is associated with the following logical volumes.

Chapter 14

Backup and Restore File System

Backup media has generally fallen into two categories. One category is tape media and the other is removable cartridge. Tape media is generally cheaper in terms of cost and supports larger sizes; however, tape media does not easily support random access to information. Removable cartridge drives, whether optical or magnetic, do support random access to information; however they have lower capacity and a much higher cost per megabyte than tape media. Finally, optical drives generally retain information for a longer time period than tapes and may be used if a permanent archival is needed

There are number of backup options available on Unix file system

Backup using CPIO

The cpio command copies files into and out from a cpio archive. The cpio archive may span multiple volumes. The -i, -o, and -p flags select the action to be performed.

cpio -i command

The cpio -i command reads from standard input an archive file created by the cpio -o command and copies from it the files with names that match the pattern parameter

The cpio -p command reads file path names from standard input and copies these files into the directory named by the   directory parameter

cpio is a copy in/out archive program, rarely used except on older System V type machines.

Examples :-

1. To copy files onto diskette, enter:

cpio -ov <filenames >/dev/rfd0

This copies the files with path names listed in the filenames file in a compact form onto the diskette (>/dev/rfd0). The v flag causes the cpio command to display the name of each file as it is copied. This command is useful for making backup copies of files. The diskette must already be formatted, but it must not contain a file system or be mounted.

2. To copy files in the current directory onto diskette, enter:

ls *.c | cpio -ov >/dev/rfd0

This copies all the files in the current directory whose names end with .c

3. To copy the current directory and all subdirectories onto diskette, enter:

find . -print | cpio -ov >/dev/rfd0

This saves the directory tree that starts with the current directory (.) and includes all of its subdirectories and files. Do this faster by entering:

find . -cpio /dev/rfd0 -print

The -print entry displays the name of each file as it is copied.

4. To list the files that have been saved onto a diskette with the cpio command, enter:

cpio -itv </dev/rfd0

Note:- This displays the table of contents of the data previously saved onto the /dev/rfd0 file in the cpio command format.

The listing is similar to the long directory listing produced by the ls -l command. To list only the file path names, use only the **-it** flags.

5. To copy the files previously saved with the cpio command from a diskette, enter:

cpio -idmv </dev/rfd0

This copies the files previously saved onto the /dev/rfd0 file by the cpio command back into the file system (specify the **-i** flag).

The **d** flag allows the cpio command to create the appropriate directories if a directory tree is saved.

The **m** flag maintains the last modification time in effect when the files are saved.

The **v** flag causes the cpio command to display the name of each file as it is copied.

6. To copy selected files from diskette, enter:

cpio -i "*.c" "*.o" </dev/rfd0

This copies the files that end with .c or .o from diskette. Note that the patterns "*.c" and "*.o" must be enclosed in quotation marks to prevent the shell from treating the * (asterisk) as a pattern-matching character. This is a special case in which the cpio command itself decodes the pattern-matching characters.

7. To rename files as they are copied from diskette, enter:

cpio -ir </dev/rfd0

The -r flag causes the cpio command to ask you whether to rename each file before copying it from diskette. For example, the message: Rename <prog.c> asks whether to give the file saved as prog.c a new name as it is copied. To rename the file, type the new name and press the Enter key. To keep the same name, you must enter the name again. To avoid copying the file at all, press the Enter key.

8. To copy a directory and all of its subdirectories, enter:

mkdir /home/jim/newdir

find . -print | cpio -pdl /home/jim/newdir

This duplicates the current directory tree, including the current directory and all of its subdirectories and files. The duplicate is placed in the new /home/jim/newdir directory.

Note:- The (i) flag causes the cpio command to link files instead of copying them, when possible.

As a DBA you may have to backup the oracle_home before patching or upgrading.

Backup ORACLE_HOME using CPIO

For example in this example ORACLE_HOME= /u01/app/oracle/product/9.2.0

Login with software owner account

cd /u01/app/oracle/product

find 9.2.0 -print|cpio -ov >/orabackup/tmp/920_bkp.cpio 2>/orabackup/tmp/920_bkp.cpio.log

Verify backup using CPIO

cd <temp dir> with 2GB free space

cd /tmp

cpio -idmv</orabackup/tmp/920_bkp.cpio >920_bkp.cpio.extract.log 2>&1

Note:- It extracts exactly the entire file structure including 9.2.0 directory under the current directory

Verify backed up files match with the original directory structure

Login as oracle and list files under /tmp and **/u01/app/oracle/product** into a file
cd /tmp
ls -lR 9.2.0 > 920files_bkp.log

cd /u01/app/oracle/product
ls -lR 9.2.0 > 920files.log
use the diff command to check the difference in two listing

diff 920files_bkp.log 920files.log >diff.lst

Note:- The diff log should only contain entries for soft links, as the new links are created with current timestamp.

Restoring files with CPIO

cd /restore_directory
It extracts all files under 9.2.0 directory under the current directory

cpio   -idmv</orabackup/tmp/920_bkp.cpio >920_bkp.cpio.extract.log 2>&1

Backup using tar

The "tar" command stands for tape archive.

This command is used to create new archives, list files in existing archives, and extract files from archives.

The tar command can be used to write archives directly to tape devices, or you can use it to create archive files on disk. In many cases, *tar archives* are created on disk so it is easier to transport them across networks, such as the Internet.

Chapter 14: Backup and Restore File System

Tape archive (tar) program is easy to use and transportable, has limit on file name size, won't backup special files, does not follow symbolic links, doesn't support multiple volumes.

Advantage is that tar is supported everywhere. Also useful for copying directories

Examples:-

1. To extract files from tar file

    $tar –xvf   filename.tar

2. To tar up all files and directories under current directory . or under "PROD1" directory and to write files to filename.tar

    $tar -cvf /tmp/filename.tar .

    $tar -cvf /tmp/filename.tar   PROD1

3. When filesize is too large (more than 8GB) , use –E option

    $tar -cvfE /data/oradata/tars/PROD1/large_file_blob.tar

4. To display only the content in tar binary file

    $tar –tvf   filename.tar

Compress files

1. To compress binary files

    $gzip filename.tar

2. To compress ASCII files

    $compress filename.html

3. To uncompress and untar the file in one command

$zcat filename.tar.Z | tar xvf –

4. To display only the content of compressed tar file

$gunzip -dc filename.tar.gz|tar -tvf –

5. To compress for about 15% of original size

$bzip2 full_exp.dmp → Slow but compresses for
about 15% of original size

6. To uncompress binary file

$gunzip file_name.dmp.gz

Backup using dump

Dump is completely different from **tar**, it is a program for backing
up and restoring file system. It backs up the entire file system - not
the files. Dump does not care what file system is on the hard drive,
or even if there are files in the file system. It examines files on an
ext2 file system, determines which ones need to be backed up, and
copies those files to a specified disk, tape, file or other storage
medium. It dumps one file system at a time quickly and efficiently.
Unfortunately, it does not do individual directories, and so it eats up
a great deal more storage space than **tar**. It is also written
specifically for backups.

dump (or rdump) reads the raw file system and copies the data
blocks out to tape.

Thus for backup of a directory tree tar or cpio is better suited. dump
backs up all files in filesystem, or files changed after a certain date
to magnetic tape or files.

The restore command performs the inverse function of dump, It can
restore a full backup of a file system. Subsequent incremental

backups can then be layered on top of the full backup. Single files and directory sub trees may also be restored from full or partial backups. You can use dump if you need a procedure for both backing up file systems and restoring file systems after backups.

Dump has several levels of backup procedures. The levels range from 0 to 9, where level number 0 means a full backup and guarantees the entire file system is copied. A level number above 0, incremental backup, tells dump to copy all files new or modified since the last dump of the same or lower level. To be more precise, at each incremental backup level you back up everything that has changed since the previous backup at the same or a previous level.

Examples:-

1. use tape 1 for the first full backup

[root@hunter] /# **dump** -0u -f /dev/st0 /home

2. use tape 2 for the incremental backups.

[root@hunter] /# **dump** -3u -f /dev/st0 /home

Where

- -0 to -9 is the backup level option you want to use.
- The u option means to update the file /etc/dumpdates after a successful dump.
- The -f option to write the backup to file

The file could be a

  i. special device file like /dev/st0, *a tape drive*,
 ii. /dev/rsd1c, *a disk drive*,
iii. An ordinary file
 iv. The standard output.

159

Restoring files with dump

[root@hunter] /# cd /home

To restore files from a dump in interactive mode, use the following command:

[root@hunter] /home]# restore -i -f /dev/st0

Part 7

Chapter 15
Unix System Parameters

Unix system has number of parameters, these parameters control the performance of the system. Quite a number of these parameters are considered to be tuneable.

Display Server Device Values

Devices connected to any given server can be found by using following commands based on the flavour of Unix.

On HP-Unix:

Using the **lsdev** command, you can display information about all the devices connected to your server. This includes disk drives, memory, CPUs, buses and other hardware components.

The lsdev command is used to list all mounted devices for a server.

>**lsdev**

On AIX:

>**lsdev –C** is used to display all the devices on the AIX server.

Display System Kernel Parameters

Certain kernel parameters, such as semmni and maxusers are critical to the successful operation of Oracle under Unix.

On HP-Unix

You can use the **kmtune** command to display all of the kernel configuration parameter settings

>**kmtune**

On AIX

You use the **lsattr** command to view settings for kernel parameters.

>**lsattr -El sys0**

This command is useful for displaying system variables, such as maxuproc and maxbuf that are used by Oracle.

HP Tru64 Unix-Based Systems

1. To determine the physical RAM size, enter the following command:

 # /bin/vmstat -P | grep "Total Physical Memory"

If the size of the physical RAM installed in the system is less than the required size, you must install more memory before continuing.

2. To determine the size of the configured swap space, enter the following command:

 # /sbin/swapon -s

If necessary, refer to your operating system documentation for information about how to configure additional swap space.

HP-UX Based Systems

1. To determine the physical RAM size, enter the following command:

 # grep "Physical:" /var/adm/syslog/syslog.log

If the size of the physical RAM installed in the system is less than the required size, you must install more memory before continuing.

2. To determine the size of the configured swap space, enter the following command:

 # /usr/sbin/swapinfo -a

AIX Based Systems

1. To determine the physical RAM size, enter the following command:

 # /usr/sbin/lsattr -E -l sys0 -a realmem

If the size of the physical RAM installed in the system is less than the required size, you must install more memory before continuing.

2. To determine the size of the configured swap space, enter the following command:

 # /usr/sbin/lsps -a

Linux based Systems

1. To determine the physical RAM size, enter the following command:

 # grep MemTotal /proc/meminfo

If the size of the physical RAM installed in the system is less than the required size, you must install more memory before continuing.

2. To determine the size of the configured swap space, enter the following command:

 # grep SwapTotal /proc/meminfo

Unix system Information

Some of the Handy commands on various flavors of Unix
System Information on Solaris

Commands	Description
prtconf –v	Displays the size of the system memory and reports information about peripheral devices
psrinfo –v	Displays information about processors
showrev -p	Reports which patches are installed
prtdiag –v	Displays system diagnostic information
scinstall –pv	Displays Sun Cluster release and package version information

Random Access Memory

To determine the amount of random access memory installed on your system, you could use the following command on different platform :

Unix Platform   Command

AIX $ /usr/sbin/lsattr -E -l sys0 –a realmem
Linux $ /usr/sbin/dmesg | grep "Physical:"
HP $ grep MemTotal /proc/meminfo
Solaris $ /usr/sbin/prtconf | grep "Memory size"
Tru64 $ /bin/vmstat -P | grep "Total Physical Memory"

Swap Space

To determine the amount of swap space currently configured in your system, enter one of the commands listed in the following table, depending on your platform:

Unix Platform	Command
AIX	$ /usr/sbin/lsps –a
Linux	$ /sbin/swapon –s
HP	$ /usr/sbin/swapinfo –a
Tru64	$ /sbin/swapon –s
Solaris	$ /usr/sbin/swap -l

Some of the handy commands

1. Check the virtual Memory

The svmon command captures a snapshot of virtual memory, so it is useful for determining which processes, user programs, and segments are consuming the most real, virtual, and paging space memory. The svmon command can also do tier and class reports on Workload Manager.

svmon -P -n -v -w -t 10 >> /tmp/top_10

2. Show Operating System Patch Level

$ showrev –p

3. Important SUN Solaris Commands

$ who -r   # Show Run Level
$ /usr/sbin/prtconf # Print the complete system configuration

$ **/sbin/mountall -l** # Mount all local filesystems.

$ **/sbin/init S**   #Changing to single user mode

4. Determine the physical RAM size

Enter the following command:

/usr/sbin/prtconf | grep "Memory size"

If the size of the physical RAM installed in the system is less than the required size, you must install more memory before continuing.

5. Determine the size of the configured swap space

Enter the following command:

/usr/sbin/swap –s

6. Determine the system architecture

/bin/isainfo –kv

7. OS patches installed on the server

$showrev –p

8. To check if a particular patch is installed

$pkginfo -i Packagename

9. nslookup (Query Internet domain name servers)

Description:-
nslookup - Query Internet name servers interactively. This utility is a program to query Internet domain name servers.

Syntax
nslookup [-Option ...] [Host] [-NameServer

For Example :-

$nslookup uiv220dedw
Server: 10.36.3.88
Address: 10.36.3.88#57

Name: univ220dedw.eau
Address: 10.137.3.128

$>nslookup pdbserver-env.srv

Server: un2004-tr0.srv
Address: 194.38.248.19

Name: **pdbserver-env.srv**
Address: 57.193.11.238

Note:- The nslookup command enters interactive mode when no arguments are given

10. netstat

Description
The netstat command displays the contents of certain network-related data structures in various formats, depending on the options you select.

Note:- As a DBA it's very handy to find out if a given port on a server is been used or not

Syntax to find if a given port number is been used

Note:- If port is not been used , the following command wouldn't return anything

$netstat -an|grep 5129

```
tcp4   0   0 192.168.3.61.5129     192.168.3.61.40431    ESTABLISHED
tcp4   0   0 192.168.3.61.40431    192.168.3.61.5129     ESTABLISHED
tcp4   0   0 192.168.31.29.5129    192.168.31.29.40430   ESTABLISHED
tcp4   0   0 192.168.31.29.40430   192.168.31.29.5129    ESTABLISHED
```

11. MKNOD Special file

DESCRIPTION

  mknod makes a directory entry for a special file.

OPTIONS

The following options are supported:

b   Create a block-type special file.

c   Create a character-type special file.

p   Create a FIFO (named pipe).

MKNOD → Create a FIFO (named pipe) which is a acronym for First in First Out.

When you want to create an export dump and when the available diskspace is limited, It is handy to create a FIFO (named pipe) which compresses the file in parallel while it's still exporting, which would enable to create compressed dump file

The Syntax to use named pipe with oracle export

$cat mknod_exp.sh
mknod_exp.sh - mknod file for export

EXP_FILE=/tmp/exp_file_name.dmp
LOG_FILE=/tmp/exp_file_name.log
PAR_FILE=/tmp/exp_file_name.par

mknod $EXP_FILE p
compress < $EXP_FILE > $EXP_FILE.Z &
exp file=$EXP_FILE log=$LOG_FILE parfile=$PAR_FILE
rm $EXP_FILE

The Syntax to use named pipe with oracle import

$cat mknod_imp.sh
mknod_imp.sh - mknod file for import

EXP_FILE=/tmp/exp_file_name.dmp
LOG_FILE=/tmp/imp_file_name.log
PAR_FILE=/tmp/imp_file_name.par

mknod $EXP_FILE p
uncompress < $EXP_FILE.Z > $EXP_FILE &
imp file=$EXP_FILE log=$LOG_FILE parfile=$PAR_FILE

12. nohup - run a command immune to hang-ups

The nohup utility invokes the named command with the arguments supplied. This utility can be used when it is known that command takes a long time to run and the user wants to log out of the terminal. nohup command runs the command/script even if connection from client is disconnected

The Syntax to use nohup :-

$nohup mknod_exp.sh > mknod_exp.log 2>&1 &

13. To redirect the output to the logfile as well as to screen at the same time

$nohup ./mknod_exp.sh | tee -a $./exp/mknod_exp.log

Note:- "tee –a" command sends output in parallel to screen and the file

14. Cron

The cron is a process that runs when the UNIX system is in multiuser mode. It runs commands on a regularly scheduled basis. Once every minute it checks the crontab file to see if something is supposed to be run. If it finds something it runs the command, otherwise it sleeps for another minute

```
# Sample crontab
# Everything on a line is separated by blanks or tabs
# min      hour      day      month     day-of-week        command
#(0-59)    (0-23)    (1-31)   (1-12)    (0-6
                                        Sunday=0
#-------------------------------------------------------------------------
0          8         *        *         1-5                /morn/alarm
45         10        17       4         *                  /taxes/3245
1          13        24       8         0,6                /work/drive
```

An asterisk (*) means do it every time

Crontab options

$>**crontab -l**   →Lists the content of crontab
$>**crontab –e**   →You can edit crontab directly
$>**crontab   filename** → Make changes to filename and run crontab command with filename as argument which will overwrite crontab entries with filename entries

Crontab entry examples:-

Redirects the log to logfile

```
05 17 * * * /u01/app/oracle/admin/mknod_exp.sh     ORACLE_SID >
/u01/app/oracle/admin/mknod_exp.log 2>&1

05 17 * * * /u01/app/oracle/admin/mknod_exp.sh   ORACLE_SID > /dev/null
2>&1
```

CRONJOB to run as different user

```
0 5 * * * su - esbe -c "/home/esbe/apps/prod1_purge/bin/production_purge.sh >
/home/esbe/apps/prod_purge/log/production_purge.out 2&>1"
```

15. Database TIMEZONE

The database time zone is relevant only for TIMESTAMP WITH LOCAL TIME ZONE columns. Oracle normalizes all TIMESTAMP WITH LOCAL TIME ZONE data to the time zone of the database when the data is stored on disk. If you do not specify the SET TIME_ZONE clause, then Oracle uses the time zone of the operating system of the server. If the operating system's time zone is not a valid Oracle time zone, then the database time zone defaults to UTC.

To find out the time zone of a database, use the `DBTIMEZONE` function as shown in the following example:

```
SQL>SELECT dbtimezone FROM dual;

DBTIME
-------
-08:00
```

Time Zone Parameters for Sessions

You can change the time zone parameter of a user session by issuing an ALTER SESSION statement:

- Operating system local time zone

  ALTER SESSION SET TIME_ZONE = local;

- Database time zone

  ALTER SESSION SET TIME_ZONE = DBTIMEZONE;

- An absolute time difference from UTC

  ALTER SESSION SET TIME_ZONE = '-05:00';

- Time zone for a named region

  ALTER SESSION SET TIME_ZONE = 'America/New_York'

Time Zone Parameters for Databases

You can create a database with a specific time zone by specifying:

- A displacement from UTC (Coordinated Universal Time, formerly Greenwich Mean Time). The following example sets the time zone of the database to Pacific Standard time (eight hours behind UTC):

CREATE DATABASE ... SET TIME_ZONE = '-08:00 ';

- The following example sets the time zone of the database to Pacific Standard time in the United States:

CREATE DATABASE ... SET TIME_ZONE = 'PST ';

To see a list of valid region names, query the **V$TIMEZONE_NAMES** view.

After the database has been created, you can change the time zone by issuing the ALTER DATABASE SET TIME_ZONE statement and then shutting down and starting up the database. The following example sets the time zone of the database to London time:

ALTER DATABASE SET TIME_ZONE = 'Europe/London ';

16. Check the Database Character Set in Oracle Databases

Query the target database to determine the value of the NLS_CHARACTER SET parameter for the database.

SELECT VALUE FROM V$NLS_PARAMETERS WHERE PARAMETER='NLS_CHARACTERSET';

VALUE

WE8MSWIN1252

SQL> SELECT * FROM NLS_DATABASE_PARAMETERS;

PARAMETER   VALUE
------------------------------ --
NLS_NCHAR_CHARACTERSET   AL16UTF16
NLS_LANGUAGE   AMERICAN
NLS_TERRITORY   AMERICA
NLS_CURRENCY $
NLS_ISO_CURRENCY   AMERICA
NLS_NUMERIC_CHARACTERS   .,
NLS_CHARACTERSET   WE8MSWIN1252
NLS_CALENDAR   GREGORIAN

```
NLS_DATE_FORMAT          DD-MON-RR
NLS_DATE_LANGUAGE          AMERICAN
NLS_SORT              BINARY
NLS_TIME_FORMAT          HH.MI.SSXFF AM
NLS_TIMESTAMP_FORMAT       DD-MON-RR HH.MI.SSXFF AM
NLS_TIME_TZ_FORMAT        HH.MI.SSXFF AM TZR
NLS_TIMESTAMP_TZ_FORMAT     DD-MON-RR HH.MI.SSXFF AM TZR
NLS_DUAL_CURRENCY       $
NLS_COMP              BINARY
NLS_LENGTH_SEMANTICS     BYTE
NLS_NCHAR_CONV_EXCP      FALSE
NLS_RDBMS_VERSION       10.2.0.3.0
```

Operating system info on Unix

To print name of current system

$uname

OPTIONS

The following options are supported:

-a Prints basic information currently available   from   the system.

-i Prints the name of the hardware implementation (plat-form).

-m Prints the machine hardware name (class). Use of this option is discouraged; use uname -p instead. See NOTES   section below.

-n Prints the nodename (the nodename is the name by which the system is known to a   communications network).

-p Prints the current host's ISA or processor type.

-r Prints the operating system release level.

-s Prints the name of the operating system. This is the default.

Semaphore Management

Semaphores are signals used by Oracle to serialize the internal Oracle processes. The number of semaphores for a database is equal to the value of the PROCESSES parameter in the INIT.ORA file. For example, a database with Processes=200 will have 200 semaphores allocated for Oracle.

Tip:- AIX Unix does not use semaphores. In AIX, the post/wait driver is used instead, because it increases performance.

It is critical that the Unix kernel parameter semmns be set to at least double the total number of processes for all database instances on your server. If it's not set, your databases will fail to start.

Display Values for Semaphores

The maximum allowed number of semaphores is specified by the semmns kernel parameter.

Note:- In HU-UX Version 11 you could use kmtune command to show Semaphores

>kmtune|grep sem

Count used Semaphores

You can use the –sa option of the ipcs command to display the number of used semaphores
>ipcs –sa|grep oracle

```
s 268435563   0xb01339c0 --ra-r-----   oracle oinstall   oracle
oinstall  254 10:14:58 12:13:51
s 251658364   0x18dd6f34 --ra-r-----   oracle oinstall   oracle
oinstall  154 10:15:08 12:13:42
s 251658288   0xd9c82438 --ra-r-----   oracle oinstall   oracle
oinstall  154 10:15:18 12:13:32
s  83886123   0xa2e5360 --ra-r-----    oracle oinstall   oracle
oinstall   74 10:06:55 12:10:41
s  67108983   0x6ca538f0 --ra-r-----   oracle oinstall   oracle
oinstall  104 10:07:51 12:10:18
```

```
s   50331720   0xccf6102c --ra-r-----   oracle oinstall   oracle
oinstall   64 10:15:23 12:08:59
s   16777342   0xf54a9dfc --ra-r-----   oracle oinstall   oracle
oinstall   254 10:15:10 12:07:03.
```

From above output sum of highlighted column would give the semaphores held by the oracle user for various instances.

Determine the Semaphore sets held by an Instance.

When you need to remove a semaphore set for a crashed instance, you cannot tell using the **ipcs −sa** command just which semaphore sets are associated with which instances.

How to check semaphores on unix server ?

Login as ROOT

On Solaris

1. sysdef|grep SHM

4294967295   max shared memory segment size (SHMMAX)
  100 shared memory identifiers (SHMMNI)

2. more /etc/system

At the end of the above file you see following entries

```
* Shared memory and Semaphore settings for Oracle
set shmsys:shminfo_shmmax=4294967295
set shmsys:shminfo_shmmin=1
set shmsys:shminfo_shmmni=100
set shmsys:shminfo_shmseg=10
set semsys:seminfo_semmni=4096
set semsys:seminfo_semmnu=4096
set semsys:seminfo_semmsl=1000
set semsys:seminfo_semmns=10240
set semsys:seminfo_semopm=100
set semsys:seminfo_semvmx=32767
```

Semaphore Parameters

Each oracle database process consumes one semaphore on unix system. Technically each database need as many semaphores as number of process parameter set in init.ora parameter file. For systems with multiple databases the number of semaphore requirement would be the sum of the PROCESSES parameter for all databases.

Though this calculated value sounds logically perfect unix in fact request enough semaphores for twice the processes specified during the database startup. For this reason it makes perfect sense to set the semaphore value relatively and reasonably high.

set   semsys:seminfo_semmni=300
*semmni sets the number of semaphore sets available

This controls the number of semaphore sets available. In an ideal world we would only need one set per database, but more realistically it is nice to have a bunch extra around.

set   semsys:seminfo_semmsl=500
*semmsl sets the number of semaphores per set

This parameter will determine how many semaphores exist in each semaphore set. Since semaphores are always allocated in sets it is most convenient if this is greater than or equal to the PROCESSES parameter for your largest database.

set   semsys:seminfo_semmns=30000
*semmns sets the total number of semaphores available

SEMMNS limits the number of semaphores which can be generated in the system. The actual number of semaphores available will actually be the lower of either SEMMNS or SEMMSL*SEMMNI.

Change Kernel Parameters

It's often necessary to make changes to kernel parameters on a Unix system in order to accommodate the needs of the Oracle database software.

Note: Always consult your documentation before changing system parameters. kernel configuration requires a great deal of expertise, and always work with your system administrator.

You could change the kernel parameters by using the following utility on various Operating System

Operating System	Utility
HP-UX	SAM
SCP	SYSADMSH
AIX	SMIT
Solaris	ADMINTOOL

Chapter 16
Memory Usage and Monitoring

Memory and CPU Management is important subject of DBA's. When database server is experiencing a CPU overload or a memory-swapping problem, no amount of Oracle tuning can relieve that. Hence it's important to check the memory and CPU as part of tuning task

The commands used to manage Memory and CPU Management differs between Unix dialects.

Display RAM Size on Unix

There are numerous tools in UNIX that allow the display and management of RAM memory.

Displaying the total RAM on the UNIX server

The following commands can be used to see how much RAM memory exists on a server, however they do not show used RAM size.

Unix dialects	Command to display RAM
Solaris	prtconf|grep -i mem
AIX	lsdev -C|grep mem
Linux	Free
DEC-UNIX	uerf -r 300	grep -i mem

Display RAM Size in Solaris

prtconf command can be used on Solaris to see the available memory.

For example:

>prtconf|grep –i mem

Display RAM Size in AIX

You can use the lsdev command followed by the lsattr command to display the amount of memory on the server.

>lsdev -C|grep mem

mem0   Available 00-00   Memory

Here you can see that mem0 is the name of the memory device, Now that you have the name, you can issue the command

>lsattr -El   to see the amount of memory on the server.

>lsattr -El mem0

Display RAM Size in HP-UX

The **glance** utility displays a screen showing CPU and memory utilization both for the system as a whole and for individual processes. The **sar** utility displays a complete set of system settings and also shows overall server performance.

Note:- In some shops, you may need to get permission from your system administrator in order to run **glance** or **sar**

Display RAM Size in DEC Unix

You could use uerf command in conjunction with grep to display memory size.
>uerf -r 300 |grep -i mem

Use svmon in AIX

The AIX dialect of Unix has a server monitor utility called svmon. The svmon utility displays a usage map of all memory on the server, including memory in use and paging space.

It captures and analyses a snapshot of virtual memory.

The svmon command displays information about the current state of memory. The displayed information does not characterize a true snapshot of memory, as svmon runs at user level, with interrupts enabled.

The **svmon** command monitors virtual memory. It determines which processes, users, programs, and segments are consuming the most real, virtual, and page space memory. The statistics reported by **svmon** are expressed in terms of pages, where a page is 4 kilobytes.

The **svmon** command can be run like **vmstat** with **intervals** and **count** to record how memory is changing over time:

svmon -i<*interval*> <*count*>

Which takes a snapshot every <*interval*> seconds for <*count*> times

Command	Result
svmon –i <interval> <count> displayed	System wide memory use is
svmon -uP -t 3 process can be determined	Most real memory usage
svmon -gP -t 3 process can be determined	Most paging space usage

182

svmon -pP *<PID>*   To find out what files a
process or command is using, where **<PID>** is the process ID
number.

svmon –gS   To find out which segments are
in paging space

#svmon

The svmon command can also be used with the –P option to display
characteristics for a specific process.

For example:-

root>svmon –P 32679

This command is especially useful if you want to see the detail
memory usage for a specific Oracle process. For example, if you
see an Oracle process that you suspect to be in a loop, use the
svmon –P command to reveal the actual memory usage for the task.
Oracle tasks that are in a memory loop will often use excessive
memory. "32679" in above example represents process id of
process in question.

Display allocated Memory Segments

ipcs

Desc:- Report inter-process communication facilities status
To see all allocated memory segments for your server, enter the ipcs
command as shown in the following example

>ipcs -pmb

The processes owned by the Oracle user are associated with the
Oracle System Global Area (SGA). To see information about the
specific memory segments allocated to an instance, you can enter

SQL*Plus as sysdba and connect to instance, and issue the oradebug ipc command

Determining which instance owns which shared memory & semaphore segments

Consider the situation where you have several instances running on one database server and one crashes leaving the "sgadef<SID>.dbf" file, shared memory and semaphore segments running. Given that you have many instances running, it becomes unclear which shared memory and semaphore sets to kill. The steps below will allow you to determine which shared memory and semaphore segments **NOT** to kill.

First, run **"ipcs -b"** on the database server.

After logging into each database instance and running "oradebug ipc", you will know which segments are valid on the running databases. Using this process of elimination you can identify the idle segments from a crashed instance. You can then kill them using **"ipcrm -m"** and **"ipcrm -s"** respectfully.

The command syntax to remove the shared memory segments or semaphores is as follows:

% ipcrm -m <shared memory id>
% ipcrm -s <semaphore id>

Running "oradebug" in Orcale 8

When running "oradebug" in an Oracle8 environment, Oracle will write all shared memory information to a trace file in your "user_dump_dest" directory while writing semaphore information to your screen. Output from "oradebug ipc" in an Oracle8 environment would look like the following:

Note:- On oracle 8i both the shared memory and semaphore information is written to the "user_dump_dest" trace file.

```
SVRMGR> connect internal
Connected.
svrmgr> oradebug ipc
Shared memory information written to trace file.
-------------------- Semaphores --------------------
Total number of semaphores = 250
Number of semaphores per set = 25
Number of semaphore sets = 10
Semaphore identifiers:
 0 65537 2 3 4 5 6 7 8 9
```

To gather information about the shared memory in the trace file, navigate to your "user_dump_dest" directory and type in "ls -lt". This will order the files by modification date. Your trace file will be at the top of the file listing

Running "oradebug" in Oracle9i

If you try "oradebug" command in oracle9i, you are likely to get ORA- error. The reason is on oracle 9i version the syntax to use this command slightly changes. You need to provide the server process id (background process on oracle) as one of the parameter to "oradebug setospid" command.

SQL> **oradebug ipc**

ORA-00074: no process has been specified

When you run in an OPS environment rather than in a single mode environment, you will need to have two telnet sessions open to the database server: One to login to SQL*Plus and second one is determine the background process (server processes) of the SQL*Plus session:

% **sqlplus "/ as sysdba"**

Now in another shell session, look for the background (sever) process of the SQL*Plus session:

% **ps -ef | grep TARGDB | grep LOCAL**

185

oracle **4744** 1 0 12:54:55 ?   0:00 oracleTARGDB
(DESCRIPTION=(LOCAL=YES)(ADDRESS=(PROTOCOL=beq)))

Now go back to your SQL*Plus session and issue the following:
> SQL> **oradebug setospid 4744**
> Statement processed.
> SQL> **oradebug ipc**
> Information written to trace file.

In Oracle9i, this change was made to support dumping IPC information for oracle Parallel Server (OPS) or RAC. Unlike semaphores and shared memory IPC information is different for every process when you run in an OPS environment rather than in a single mode environment.

Following is a workaround to obtain shared memory and semaphore information in Oracle9i.

In this example, you will need to have two telnet sessions open to the database server: One to login to SQL*Plus and another to determine the background process (server processes) of the SQL*Plus session:

% sqlplus "/ as sysdba"

Now in another shell session, look for the background (sever) process of the SQL*Plus session:

% ps -ef | grep TARGDB | grep LOCAL

oracle **6321** 1 0 12:54:55 ?   0:00 oracleTARGDB
(DESCRIPTION=(LOCAL=YES)(ADDRESS=(PROTOCOL=beq)))

Now go back to your SQL*Plus session and issue the following:
> SQL> **oradebug setospid 6321**
> Statement processed.

> SQL> **oradebug ipc**

Information written to trace file.

Manually De allocate a Memory Segment

When an Oracle instance crashes, sometimes its memory segments are still held as allocated by the server. When this happens, they must be manually de allocated. One way to do this is to use the ipcrm command, passing in the segment ID as an argument. You can get the segment ID from the ipcs command output. For example, the following command de allocates segment ID 234532

>ipcrm
desc :-   ipcrm - remove a message queue, semaphore set, or shared   memory ID
-m shmid   Removes the shared memory identifier shmid from the system.
-q msqid   Removes the message queue identifier msqid from the system and destroys the message queue and data structure associated with it.
-s semid   Removes the semaphore identifier semid from the system and destroys the set of sema-phores and data structure associated with it.

>ipcrm −m 234532

Note:- It's easy to clobber SGA for a running instance with the ipcrm . Only use this command when the background process for an instance have abnormally died.

Displaying the number of CPU processors in UNIX

You need to have special command for each dialect of UNIX to display CPU information. Knowing the number of CPUs is very important to the Oracle DBA because it shows the number of parallel query processes that can be concurrently executing on the UNIX server.

Commands to display number of CPU

UNIX Dialect	Command to display the number of CPUs
Linux	cat /proc/cpuinfo|grep processor|wc –l
Solaris	psrinfo -v|grep "Status of processor"|wc –l
AIX	lsdev -C|grep Process|wc –l
HP/UX	ioscan -C processor | grep processor | wc - l

Display the number of CPUs on AIX

The **lsdev** command can be used to see the number of CPUs on a server. This is very important, because it shows the number of parallel query processes that can be used on that server. That in turn limits the value that you can use following the DEGREE keyword in a parallel query or DML statement.

Following command on AIX server shows, server has four CPU's
>**lsdev -C|grep Process |wc –l**

4

Display the number of CPUs in Solaris

On solaris, the prsinfo command can be used to count the number of CPUs on the server.

For example:

>**psrinfo -v|grep "Status of processor"|wc –l**

or

>**psrinfo   -v|grep   "Status   of   virtual processor"|wc –l**

To see details about the CPUs, you can use the –v (verbose) option:

>**psrinfo –v**

System Configuration and diagnostic information

/usr/sbin/prtdiag -v

Description:-

prtdiag displays system configuration and diagnostic information on sun4u and sun4v systems.

The diagnostic information lists any failed field replaceable units (FRUs) in the system.

Note:- The interface, output, and location in the directory hierarchy for prtdiag are uncommitted and subject to change in future releases.

Chapter 17
Load Monitoring on
Unix Server

To effectively monitor a given database comprises of monitoring of database as well as the database server that hosts the database.

For database server monitoring there are number of Unix commands available, which displays CPU and memory consumption. Common utilities include **top, sar and vmstat**

Performance Monitoring, CPU usage and Processes

Using top

One of the popular Load monitoring command on Unix is **top**. The top command shows the relative activity for each CPU in the CPU cluster.

The output from top is in 2 sections. The first section shows the average load on entire server, while the second section lists the current top sessions in terms of CPU utilization.

1. Average load on Server.
2. Current top sessions in terms of CPU utilization.

Here is the sample output from top command

>**top**

load averages: 10.55, 11.49, 11.89
10:37:41
2253 processes:2249 sleeping, 2 stopped, 2 on cpu
CPU states: 63.8% idle, 12.7% user, 23.5% kernel, 0.0%
iowait, 0.0% swap
Memory: 128G real, 32G free, 88G swap in use, 35G swap free

PID USERNAME LWP PRI NICE SIZE RES STATE TIME CPU COMMAND

20837 oracle 20 49 0 0K 0K sleep 674.5H 5.22% oracle

157 oracle 20 25 0 0K 0K sleep 126.1H 1.32% oracle

```
25652 oracle  12 59  2  0K   0K sleep  54:50 0.33%
oracle
28448 oracle   1  1   0  0K   0K sleep  95:16 0.31%
oracle
24327 oracle   1 59   0  10M 7888K cpu/18  0:02 0.31%
top
28469 oracle   1  1   0  0K   0K sleep  89:24 0.28%
oracle
25862 oracle   1 59   0  0K   0K sleep  36.2H 0.26%
oracle
24048 oracle   1 36   2  0K   0K sleep  15:42 0.25%
oracle
21845 oracle  11 19   0  0K   0K sleep   0:04 0.24%
oracle

11345 oracle   1 57   2  0K   0K sleep   3:59 0.23%
oracle
16281 oracle   1  1   2  0K   0K sleep  51:05 0.23%
oracle
2793 oracle    1  9   0  0K   0K sleep  24.2H 0.22% oracle
```

At the top of the list you see 3 values for the load average, for last minute, past 5 minutes and past 15 minutes

The load average is an arbitrary number that describes the load on the system. The first load average value is the immediate load for the last minute. The next value represents the load average for the past 5 minutes. The third value is the load average for the past 15 minutes.

The second section of top output, which details the current top sessions in terms of CPU utilization.

The second part of the top output shows the top sessions. The Information such as process ID (PID), the username, the dispatching priority (PRD), the nice value (NI), the size of each task's memory (SIZE), the state, the execution time, and the percentage of CPU being used by each process is displayed in second part of the section.

Though top has many columns of information, there are only a few that are of interest to DBA's.

Load Average:-

These are the load averages for the entire server.

CPU:-
The first section of the top output shows a load summary for CPU. The CPU column in the detailed listing shows which CPU is servicing each individual task.

IDLE:-
The Idle column shows the percentage of time that each CPU has been idle.

Using sar

The sar utility (System Activity Reporter) is quite popular in SVR4 environments such as HP-UX and Solaris. It is also becoming widely available for AIX.

The sar utility samples cumulative activity counters in the operating system

You will be able to see the overall consumption of CPU, disk, memory, and Journal File System (JFS) buffer usage using this utility.

To capture CPU, swapping and buffer activity on the server, you could use three flags with sar and they are

CPU activity
>sar –u

Shows CPU activity

Swapping activity
>sar -w

Shows swapping activity

Buffer activity
>sar –b

Shows buffer activity

The output from a sar report usually shows a time-based snapshot of activity. In simple form of sar command usage, you pass two numeric arguments. The first represents the time interval between samples and the second represents the number of samples to take

> sar –u 15 3

The sar command in this example is requesting three samples taken at 15-second intervals.

SunOS un128dora 5.10 Generic_141414-07 sun4u   02/04/2010

14:41:56	%usr	%sys	%wio	%idle
14:42:12	50	42	0	8
14:42:27	54	38	0	7
14:42:43	43	31	0	26
Average	49	37	0	14

CPU report using sar command

>sar –u

Overall CPU consumption over time can be seen using sar –u command. CPU time can be allocated into the following four buckets: user mode, system mode, waiting on I/O, and idle.

> sar -u 15 3

SunOS un128dora 5.10 Generic_141414-07 sun4u   02/04/2010

14:41:56	%usr	%sys	%wio	%idle
14:42:12	50	42	0	8

14:42:27	54	38	0	7
14:42:43	43	31	0	26

Average	49	37	0	14

Swapping and memory switching activity using sar

>sar – w

This command is quite handy when you suspect that your database server is experiencing a memory shortage.

When Oracle server's real memory runs short, segments of RAM are swapped out to a swap disk. Page out operations happen frequently. However page-in indicates that the Oracle server is exceeding the amount of RAM. There are two ways you could overcome the swapping issue, One is by reducing the SGA and secondly by adding more RAM for the database server.

sar –w command can be used to check the swapping activity on the database server. Both arguments represent the time interval between samples and the number of samples respectively.

> **> sar -w 6 6**

SunOS un128dora 5.10 Generic_141414-07 sun4u 02/04/2010

14:45:13	swpin/s	bswin/s	swpot/s	bswot/s	pswch/s
14:45:21	0.00	0.0	0.00	0.0	19664
14:45:28	0.00	0.0	0.00	0.0	23366
14:45:36	0.00	0.0	0.00	0.0	20341
14:45:43	0.00	0.0	0.00	0.0	22037
14:45:51	0.00	0.0	0.00	0.0	20457
14:45:58	0.00	0.0	0.00	0.0	23961

Average	0.00	0.0	0.00	0.0	21439

The columns have the following meanings:

swpin/s
Number of process swap-ins per second

swpot/s
Number of process swap-outs per second
bswin/s
Number of 512-byte swap-ins per second

bswot/s
Number of 512-byte swap–outs per second

pswch/s
Number of process context switches per second

Buffer activity report using sar command

>sar –b

When you suspect that your database is I/O bound, sar –b command can be used to report buffer activity, which equates to disk I/O activity. The report shows real disk I/O and the interaction with the Unix Journal File System (JFS) buffer.

For example :-

>sar -b 2 6

SunOS un128dora 5.10 Generic_141414-07 sun4u   02/04/2010

14:47:40	bread/s	lread/s	%rcache	bwrit/s	lwrit/s	%wcache	pread/s	pwrit/s
14:47:43	0	8659	100	213	2588	92	0	0
14:47:45	0	9222	100	238	2853	92	0	0
14:47:48	0	20018	100	281	3295	91	1	0
14:47:51	0	8118	100	122	1427	91	0	0
14:47:54	0	13598	100	247	3073	92	0	0
14:47:56	0	10982	100	200	2517	92	0	0
Average	0	11372	100	212	2559	92	0	0

Iread/s
Number of reads per second from the Unix JFS buffer cache

%rcache
Buffer cache hit ratio (for the Unix JFS buffer cache) for read requests.

bwrit/s
Number of physical writes to disk per second

lwrit/s
Number of writes per second to the Unix JFS buffer cache.

%wcache
Buffer cache hit ratio (for the Unix JFS buffer cache) for write requests.

pread/s
Number of reads per second from disk.

pwrit/s
Number of writes per second to disk.

prstat

DESCRIPTION

The prstat utility iteratively examines all active processes on the system and reports statistics based on the selected output mode and sort order. prstat provides options to examine only processes matching specified PIDs, UIDs, zone IDs, CPU IDs, and processor set IDs

If you do not specify an option, prstat examines all processes and reports statistics sorted by CPU usage.

Note:- Top most would be the one with highest CPU

Example:-
$prstat

 PID USERNAME   SIZE   RSS STATE PRI NICE   TIME **CPU**
PROCESS/NLWP

```
14914 oracle   465M 428M cpu1   0   0 33:40:24 22% oracle/11
 5057 oracle   465M 428M cpu2   0   0 44:39:43 21% oracle/11
26740 oracle   465M 428M sleep 59   0  0:00:10 3.0% oracle/1
20195 root     18M 6448K run    0   0  1:08:13 0.4% scopeux/1
27200 oracle   463M 422M sleep 59   0  0:00:00 0.4% oracle/1
26659 oracle   465M 428M sleep 59   0  0:00:05 0.2% oracle/1
24257 oracle   625M 588M sleep 52   0  0:02:05 0.2% oracle/11
27277 oracle   19M 5808K sleep 19   0  0:00:00 0.2% perl/1
22763 oracle   465M 428M sleep 59   0  0:00:36 0.2% oracle/1
27244 oracle   622M 584M sleep 59   0  0:00:00 0.1% oracle/1
27147 oracle   462M 424M sleep 59   0  0:00:00 0.1% oracle/1
```

$ps –ef|grep 14914

vmstat

Vmstat utility is the most common Unix monitoring utility. The first numeric argument to vmstat represents the time interval expressed in seconds.

The **vmstat** command reports statistics about kernel threads, virtual memory, disks, traps and CPU activity. Reports generated by the vmstat command can be used to balance system load activity. These system-wide statistics (among all processors) are calculated as averages for values expressed as percentages, and as sums otherwise.

In the example that follows, the statement vmstat 3 get a line of output every three seconds.

> **vmstat 3**

```
kthr    memory      page      disk    faults   cpu
r b w  swap free re  mf pi po fr de sr m1 m1 m1 m1  in  sy
cs us sy id
3 1 0 45683320 39352760 3282 5186 17156 29 27 0 0 0 0 0 9
5796 89441 21436 27 23 50
12 0 0 35992048 29344448 359 3688 28 8 8 0 0 0 0 0  0 3158
53063 9910 18 29 52
3 0 0 35995408 29346816 25 605 114 0 0 0 0 0  0  0  9 2735
42541 8995 15 25 60
```

199

```
0 0 0 35994648 29345480 547 3321 3074 0 0 0 0 0 0 0 0 1779
53382 9969 16 8 76
0 0 0 35991744 29342576 5 1422 97 2 2 0 0  0  0  0  0 2980
73531 11217 20 9 71
18 1 0 35989320 29339736 24 1359 0 0 0 0 0 0  0  0 10 3010
63226 9366 22 23 55
0 0 0 35991328 29341928 70 1127 132 0 0 0 0 0 0  0  0 3126
49045 10324 15 24 61
0 0 0 35990288 29340480 164 2562 761 0 0 0 0 0 0 0  0 1530
49915 9206 13 7 81
```

You can exit vmstat at any time by pressing Ctrl-C.

If the Interval parameter is not specified, the vmstat command generates a single report and then exits. The Interval parameter specifies the amount of time in seconds between each report. The first report contains statistics for the time since system startup. Subsequent reports contain statistics collected during the interval since the previous report.

The critical values you need to know are as follows:

r   This represents run queue. When run queue exceeds the number of CPUs, it's an indication that the server is experiencing a CPU bottleneck. You can get the number of CPUs by entering lsdev –C|grep process |wc –l

pi   This represents page-in count. Non-zero values typically indicate that the server is short on memory and that RAM is being written to the swap disk. However non-zero values can also occur when numerous programs are accessing memory for the first time. To find out which is the case, check the scan rate (sr) column. If both the page-in count and the scan rate are non-zero, then it is an indication of shortage of RAM.

sr The scan rate. If you see the scan rate rising steadily you know that the paging daemon is busy allocating memory pages.

Note:- For AIX and HP-UX, vmstat also provides the following CPU values. These values are expressed as percentages and will sum to 100:

us user CPU percentage
sy System CPU percentage
id Idle CPU percentage
wa Wait CPU percentage

When the sum of user and system CPU percentage (us+sy) approaches 100, it is an indication that CPUs are busy, but not necessarily overloaded. The run queue value can indicate a CPU overload, but only when the run queue exceeds the number of CPUs on the server.

For example :-

When wait CPU percentages (the wa values) exceed 25, then 25% or more of the processing time is waiting for a resource, usually I/O. It is common to see high wait CPU percentages, during backups and exports, but they can also indicate an I/O bottleneck.

Note:- Server activity can be collected over given period of time and can be stored in a table which would be useful to analyse the server performance. This can be done by automating the vmstat collection

Syntax to use vmstat

$vmstat 2 5

2 — Is the intervals
5 —-Is the no. of time display

```
kthr    memory         page              faults    cpu
----- ----------- ------------------------ ------------ -----------
 r b   avm    fre  re pi po fr  sr cy in  sy    cs  us sy id wa
 4 2 2057309 1031684  0  0  0 326 2137  0 2188 15940 8746 28 20 50  3
 2 2 2057342 1031700  0  0  0 1029 2790  0 2536 55829 3999 17 15 54 14
 2 3 2057312 1031602  0  0  0 1238 2937  0 2303 41181 3755 24  7 56 12
 3 3 2059151 1029840  0  0  0 1303 4330  0 1754 53119 2890 32 17 43  8
 4 2 2057615 1031470  0  0  0 592 2282  0 1944 66617 5439 30 26 35  8
```

Show Server Load Average

Another way of showing Oracle process usage is to monitor the load average. As mentioned before, the load average is an arbitrary number describing the load on the system.

The Unix **w (watch)** command is used to generate an abbreviated top sessions output. Watch command is very handy to quickly check server load, and good news is W is present in almost all dialects of Unix.

```
>w
 3:30pm  up 45 day(s), 12:51,  28 users,  load average: 7.55,
8.55, 9.14
User    tty        login@ idle  JCPU  PCPU  what
oracle  pts/1      1:30pm  9           -ksh
oracle  pts/2      12:19pm  7          -ksh
oracle  pts/3      10:58am 3:31   18      -ksh
oracle  pts/4      4Aug08        22   22 -ksh
oracle   pts/8      Mon 9am          6     2  ssh -l oracle
un128dora
```

Note:- You see three values for the load average (which follows the time and user count). These are the load averages for the past minute (7.55), the past 5 minutes (8.55) and the past 15 minutes (9.14)

iostat

The **iostat** command is used for monitoring system input/output device loading by observing the time the devices are active in relation to their average transfer rates. The **iostat** command generates reports that can be used to change system configuration to better balance the input/output load between physical disks.

The **iostat** command generates two types of reports, the CPU Utilization report and the Device Utilization report.

CPU Utilization Report

For multiprocessor systems, the CPU values are global averages among all processors. The report has the following format:

%user
Show the percentage of CPU utilization that occurred while executing at the user level (application).

%nice
Show the percentage of CPU utilization that occurred while executing at the user level with nice priority.

%sys
Show the percentage of CPU utilization that occurred while executing at the system level (kernel).

%iowait
Show the percentage of time that the CPU or CPUs were idle during which the system had an outstanding disk I/O request.

%idle
Show the percentage of time that the CPU or CPUs were idle and the system did not have an outstanding disk I/O request.

Device Utilization Report

The device report provides statistics on a per physical device or partition basis.

Device: This column gives the device (or partition) name
Blk_read/s
Indicate the amount of data read from the drive expressed in a number of blocks per second.
Blk_wrtn/s
Indicate the amount of data written to the drive expressed in a number of blocks per second.
Blk_read

The total number of blocks read.

Blk_wrtn

The total number of blocks written.

The important column in the **iostat output** are:-

kB_read/s

Indicate the amount of data read from the drive expressed in kilobytes per second. Data displayed are valid only with kernels 2.4 and newer.

kB_wrtn/s

Indicate the amount of data written to the drive expressed in kilobytes per second. Data displayed are valid only with kernels 2.4 and newer.

iostat display a single history since boot report for all CPU and Devices.

iostat -d 2

Display a continuous device report at two second intervals.

iostat -d 2 6

Display six reports at two second intervals for all devices.

iostat utility is a great tool for finding busy disks. When vmstat utility reports wait CPU percentage (the wa column) to indicate an I/O bottleneck, next step should be running iostat utility. I/O bottlenecks are identified by wait queues for access to the disk. Busy disks can be identified by checking iostat for high *read/write* activity. Next step would be to identify the corresponding mount point (mapping of disk to mount points can be obtained from system administrator).

Once you have identified the hot spot mount point, you can run Oracle's utlbstat –utlestat scripts or equivalent of these scripts to determine the specific oracle data files that are causing the bottleneck. Once you identify them, you can move them to less busy filesystem, or stripe the disk across several devices.

Chapter 18
Useful scripts for Oracle DBA

1. Temporary tablespace usage monitoring

Script name :-tmp_usage.sql
Desc :- This script is useful to find the total temp space currently used and the number of users using the tempspace along with maximum usage.

```
col "TABLESPACE NAME" for a15
PROMPT TEMPORARY TABLESPACE USAGE
PROMPT ----------------------------

SELECT a.tablespace_name "TABLESPACE NAME",
    round(to_number(b.value)*total_blocks/(1024*1024),2) TOTAL,
    round(to_number(b.value)*used_blocks/(1024*1024),2) USED,
    round(to_number(b.value)*free_blocks/(1024*1024),2) FREE ,
    round(to_number(b.value)*max_used_blocks/(1024*1024),2) "MAX USED",
    current_users "ACTIVE USERS"
from v$sort_segment a, v$parameter b
where b.name = 'db_block_size'
/
```

SQL>@tmp_usage.sql

```
TEMPORARY TABLESPACE USAGE
----------------------------

TABLESPACE NAME    TOTAL    USED    FREE  MAX USED ACTIVE USERS
--------------- ---------- ---------- ---------- --------- ------------------------------------------
TEMP               10000    12     9988   1407        12

SQL>
```

2. Unix wrapper to check Single database

Script name :-db_check.sql

Desc :- This script is usefull to query a given database and run multiple scripts within database from a unix script. Wrapping sql commands within unix commands help to schedule the script through cron.

```
#!/bin/ksh
#set -x
export ORACLE_SID=TESTDB
echo $ORACLE_SID
export ORAENV_ASK=NO;
. /opt/oracle/product/10.2.3/bin/oraenv ;
echo $ORACLE_HOME
echo $ORACLE_SID
TEMPFILE=/tmp/user_mon.log
sqlplus -s '/ as sysdba' <<OEM >>$TEMPFILE
set lines 132 pages 0 feed off
select to_char(sysdate,'DD-MON-YY:HH24:MI:SS') from dual;
select name, open_mode from v\$database;
@/tmp/script.sql
OEM
exit;
```

3. Unix wrapper to check Multiple database

Script name :-db_check_multiple.sql
Desc :- This script is usefull to query all database on the server for a given oracle home and run multiple scripts within database from a unix script. Wrapping sql commands within unix commands help to schedule the script through cron.

```
##########################################
# Get list of databases on the server
####################################
export TARGET_NODE=prodserver
cat /etc/oratab|grep -i "10.2.3"|awk -F: '{print $1}'|grep -v "#"
>/tmp/config/dblist_${TARGET_NODE}
cat /etc/oratab|grep -i "9.2.6"|awk -F: '{print $1}'|grep -v "#"
>>/tmp/config/dblist_${TARGET_NODE}
DB_LIST=/tmp/config/dblist_${TARGET_NODE}; export DB_LIST
echo $DB_LIST
PATH=$PATH:/usr/local/bin;export PATH
###Loop every oracle sid through for loop
for ORACLE_SID in `cat "$DB_LIST"`
do
echo $ORACLE_SID
export ORAENV_ASK=NO;
. /usr/local/bin/oraenv;
echo "You have entered $ORACLE_SID"
echo $ORACLE_HOME
```

```
TEMPFILE=/tmp/chk_db.log
sqlplus -s '/ as sysdba' <<OEM >>$TEMPFILE
set lines 132 pages 0 feed off
select to_char(sysdate,'DD-MON-YY:HH24:MI:SS') from dual;
select name, open_mode  from v\$database;
@/tmp/script.sql
OEM
done
exit;
```

4. Actual Database size used

Script name :-db_size_actual.sql
Desc :- This script is usefull to find the actual database size

```
SELECT (SPTOTAL - SPFREE) SPBACKUPGB
FROM  (SELECT SUM(DF.BYTES) SPTOTAL FROM DBA_DATA_FILES DF,
DBA_TABLESPACES TS WHERE
DF.TABLESPACE_NAME=TS.TABLESPACE_NAME),
(SELECT SUM(FR.BYTES) SPFREE FROM DBA_FREE_SPACE FR,
DBA_TABLESPACES T WHERE
FR.TABLESPACE_NAME=T.TABLESPACE_NAME)
/
```

@db_size_actual.sql

```
SPBACKUPGB
----------
1.2301E+11
```

5. Allocated space to database

```
SQL> select sum(bytes/1024/1024) ALLOCDBGB from dba_data_files;

 ALLOCDBGB
----------
   138309
```

Open Cursors

Monitoring open cursors

v$open_cursor shows *cached* cursors, *not* currently open cursors, by session. It shows the cursors in the session cursor cache for each session, *not* cursors that are actually open.

To monitor open cursors, query v$sesstat where name='opened cursors current'. This will give the number of currently opened cursors, by session:

6. Currently opened cursors

Script name :-Open_cursors.sql
Desc :- This script is usefull to find the total cursors open, by session

```
select a.value, s.username, s.sid, s.serial#
from v$sesstat a, v$statname b, v$session s
where a.statistic# = b.statistic#  and s.sid=a.sid
and b.name = 'opened cursors current';
```

7. Cursors open by username & Machine

Script name :-open_cursors_username_machine.sql
Desc :- If you're running several N-tiered applications with multiple webservers, you may find it useful to monitor open cursors by username and machine:

```
select sum(a.value) total_cur, avg(a.value) avg_cur, max(a.value) max_cur,
s.username, s.machine
from v$sesstat a, v$statname b, v$session s
where a.statistic# = b.statistic#  and s.sid=a.sid
and b.name = 'opened cursors current'
group by s.username, s.machine
order by 1 desc;
```

8. Find SQL statement associated with cached cursors

Script name :- sql_associated_with_open_cursor.sql
Desc :- This script is useful to find session cached cursors by SID and includes the first few characters of the sql statement.

```
select c.user_name, c.sid, sql.sql_text
from v$open_cursor c, v$sql sql
where c.sql_id=sql.sql_id
and c.sid=&sid;
```

9. Datafile Corruption investigation

Script name :- datafile_corruption.sql
Desc :- When you see ORA-01578, ORA-01110 errors in alert log
it's an indication that there is datafile corruption in the database.
Following script identifies the segment associated with corruption
under file_id =7 and block number 982766

Errors in file /data/prod/proddb1/bdump/proddb_smon_6260.trc:
ORA-01578: ORACLE data block corrupted (file # 7, block #
982766)
ORA-01110: data file 7:
'/data/prod/oradata/proddb1/MNT_IDX01.dbf'

```
SELECT  segment_name , segment_type , owner , tablespace_name
        FROM  sys.dba_extents
        WHERE  file_id = 7
        AND  982766 BETWEEN block_id and block_id + blocks –1;
```

SEGMENT_NAME	SEGMENT_TYPE	OWNER	TABLESPACE_NAME
IX01_MNT_DB2_TSV	INDEX PARTITION	CRM	MNT_IDX

10. Find table High water mark

A table's HWM can be calculated using the results from the
following SQL statements. First querying without analysing the
table and then analysing the table followed by querying the table.
The difference of result (clocks-empty_blocks) would give HWM

```
SELECT BLOCKS FROM  DBA_SEGMENTS WHERE
OWNER=UPPER('owner') AND SEGMENT_NAME = UPPER('table');

ANALYZE TABLE owner.table ESTIMATE STATISTICS;
```

Chapter 18: Useful scripts for Oracle DBA

SELECT EMPTY_BLOCKS FROM DBA_TABLES WHERE
OWNER=UPPER('owner') AND TABLE_NAME = UPPER('table');

Thus, the tables' HWM = (query result 1) - (query result 2) - 1

Note:- You can also use the DBMS_SPACE package and calculate the
HWM = TOTAL_BLOCKS - UNUSED_BLOCKS – 1

11. Capture SID and serial# for a given database user to kill sessions

Script name :- mk_kill_users.sql
Desc:- This script generates a list of sid and serial numbers for a
given user, which can be run to terminate all sessions run by a given
user within the database. Substitute the username with valid
database username

```
select 'alter system kill session '||''''||sid||','||serial#||''''||';' from v$session where
username ='username' ;
```

12. Backup ORACLE_HOME using CPIO

Script name:- backup_cpio.sh
Desc:- The cpio command copies files into and out from a cpio
archive. It's handy to backup oracle home before upgrade

For example in this example ORACLE_HOME=
/u01/app/oracle/product/9.2.0

Login with software owner account

cd /u01/app/oracle/product

**find 9.2.0 -print|cpio -ov >/orabackup/tmp/920_bkp.cpio
2>/orabackup/tmp/920_bkp.cpio.log**

Verify backup using CPIO

cd <temp dir> with 2GB free space

cd /tmp

cpio -idmv</orabackup/tmp/920_bkp.cpio >920_bkp.cpio.extract.log 2>&1

Note:- It extracts exactly the extire filestructure including 9.2.0 directory under the current directory

Verify backed up files match with the original directory structure

Login as oracle and list files under /tmp and
/u01/app/oracle/product into a file
cd /tmp

ls -lR 9.2.0 > 920files_bkp.log

cd /u01/app/oracle/product
ls -lR 9.2.0 > 920files.log
use the diff command to check the difference in two listing

diff 920files_bkp.log 920files.log >diff.lst

Note:- The diff log should only contain entries for soft links, as the new links are created with current timestamp.

13. Restoring files with CPIO

Script name:- restore_cpio.sh
Desc:- This script restores files from the backup to a directory 9.2.0

cd /restore_directory
It extracts all files under 9.2.0 directory under the current directory

cpio -idmv</orabackup/tmp/920_bkp.cpio >920_bkp.cpio.extract.log 2>&1

14. Backup using tar

Desc :- The "tar" command stands for tape archive.

The tar command can be used to write archives directly to tape devices, or you can use it to create archive files on disk

Note:- tape archive (tar) program is easy to use and transportable. has limit on file name size, won't backup special files, does not follow symbolic links, doesn't support multiple volumes.

Advantage is that tar is supported everywhere. Also useful for copying directories

1. To extract files from tar file

    tar –xvf   filename.tar

2. To tar up all files and directories under current directory . or under "PROD1"   directory and writes files to filename.tar

    tar -cvf /tmp/filename.tar .
    tar -cvf /tmp/filename.tar   PROD1

3. When filesize is too large (more than 8GB) , **use –E option**

    $tar -cvfE /data/oradata/tars/PROD1/large_file_blob.tar

4. To display only the content in tar binary file

    $tar –tvf   filename.tar

15. Statspack Collection Level

STATSPACK has two types of collection options, level and threshold. The *level* parameter controls the type of data collected from Oracle, while the *threshold* parameter acts as a filter for the collection of SQL statements into the *stats$sql_summary* table.

> SQL> **SELECT * FROM stats$level_description ORDER BY snap_level;**

Level 0 This level captures general statistics, including rollback segment, row cache, SGA, system events, background events, session events, system statistics, wait statistics, lock statistics, and Latch information.

Level 5 This level includes capturing high resource usage SQL Statements, along with all data captured by lower levels.

Level 6 This level includes capturing SQL plan and SQL plan usage information for high resource usage SQL Statements, along with all data captured by lower levels.

Level 7 This level captures segment level statistics, including logical and physical reads, row lock, itl and buffer busy waits, along with all data captured by lower levels.

Level 10 This level includes capturing Child Latch statistics, along with all data captured by lower levels.

You can change the default level of a snapshot with the statspack.snap function. The i_modify_parameter => 'true' changes the level permanent for all snapshots in the future.

SQL> **exec statspack.snap(i_snap_level => 6, i_modify_parameter => 'true');**

16. Set tracing on/off

Set trace on
To enable the SQL trace facility for your instance, set the value of the SQL_TRACE initialization parameter to TRUE. Statistics are collected for all sessions.

ALTER SYSTEM SET SQL_TRACE = true;

After the SQL trace facility has been enabled for the instance, you can disable it for the instance by entering:
ALTER SYSTEM SET SQL_TRACE = false;

Session level trace

To Start Tracing

```
conn sys/&&syspwd
set echo on
alter system set timed_statistics=true;
select username,osuser,sid,serial# from v$session where username =
upper('&user');
EXECUTE dbms_system.set_sql_trace_in_session(&SID,&SERIAL,TRUE);
set echo off
```

To Stop Tracing

```
-- user select username,osuser,sid,serial# from v$session;
-- MUST RUN AS SYS
accept syspwd char prompt "Enter sys password (hidden) >" Hide

conn sys/&&syspwd
set echo on
select username,osuser,sid,serial# from v$session where username =
upper('&user');
EXECUTE dbms_system.set_sql_trace_in_session(&SID,&SERIAL,FALSE);
alter system set timed_statistics=false;
set echo off
```

17. Autorace utility for SQLTuning

Using Autotrace

Note:-By default this executes the sql along with the stats collection and explain plan

This is activated in a SQL * plus session by

SQL > set autotrace on

Run the sql statement for explain plan and execution stats display

SQL>sqltune.sql

The sample explain plan and statistics would look like the following

Execution Plan
```
----------------------------------------------------------
  0    SELECT STATEMENT Optimizer=CHOOSE
  1  0  SORT (ORDER BY)
  2  1    TABLE ACCESS (FULL) OF 'JOB$'
```

Statistics
```
----------------------------------------------------------
      0 recursive calls
      4 db block gets
      1 consistent gets
      0 physical reads
      0 redo size
   1975 bytes sent via SQL*Net to client
    426 bytes received via SQL*Net from client
      2 SQL*Net roundtrips to/from client
      1 sorts (memory)
      0 sorts (disk)
      9 rows processed
```

Set autotrace on has the four additional options

SQL>set autotrace on

Option	Description
on	Displays query results, Execution plan and statistics
on statistics :	Displays the query results and statistics but no execution plan.
on explain:	Displays query results and execution plan but no statistics
traceonly:	Displays the execution plan and the statistics, but no query results.
traceonly statistics:	Displays the statistics only, no

| | execution plan or query results |
| off: | Turns off the Autotrace utility. |

18. Explain plan fo SQL tuning

To explain plan for any sql

SQL>explain plan for "sql statement"
For example

SQL>explain plan for select * from tab;

SQL> **select * from table (dbms_xplan.display);**

```
PLAN_TABLE_OUTPUT
-----------------------------------------------------------------------------------------------------
------------------------------------------------------------
| Id  | Operation          | Name   | Rows  | Bytes | Cost |
------------------------------------------------------------
|  0 | SELECT STATEMENT    |        | 11946 |  979K| 5086 |
|  1 | NESTED LOOPS OUTER  |        | 11946 |  979K| 5086 |
|  2 |  TABLE ACCESS FULL  | OBJ$   | 11946 |  886K|  578 |
|  3 |  TABLE ACCESS CLUSTER| TAB$  |    1 |    8 |    1 |
|  4 |   INDEX UNIQUE SCAN | I_OBJ# |    1 |      |    0 |
------------------------------------------------------------
```

19. Softlink creation

To create softlink under $ORACLE_HOME/dbs directory

cd $ORACLE_HOME/dbs

ln –s /opt/oracle/admin/PRODSID1/pfile/initPRODSID1.ora   initPRODSID1.ora

Where /opt/oracle/admin/PRODSID1/pfile is the physical location of the file

ls -l initPRODSID1.ora -> /opt/oracle/admin/PRODSID1/pfile/initPRODSID1.ora

20. dot profile   (.profile)

Sample dot profile would look like

```
# Aliases
#
set history=100
alias alert='tail –100\
 $DBA/$ORACLE_SID/bdump/alert_$ORACLE_SID.log|more'
alias sid='echo $ORACLE_SID;PS1=`echo $ORACLE_SID`"> "'
alias arch='cd $ORA_DBA/$ORACLE_SID/arch'
alias bdump='cd $ORA_DBA/$ORACLE_SID/bdump'
alias cdump='cd $ORA_DBA/$ORACLE_SID/cdump'
alias pfile='cd $ORA_DBA/$ORACLE_SID/pfile'
alias rm='rm -i'
alias sid='env|grep ORACLE_SID'
alias pss='ps -ef |grep oracle |pg'
```

21. Useful unix Scripts constructs

Sometimes it's   convenient to execute SQL commands directly from the Unix prompt, without having to enter SQL*Plus each time. Following script serves as a unix wrapper template to include/run any sql scripts from Unix prompt

1. Connecting to SQLPLUS syntax

```
sqlplus -s '/ as sysdba' <<OEM | egrep -v "ERROR:|ORA-" >> $TEMPFILE
set lines 500 pagesize 0
set head off feedback off
col file_name format a500
select file_name from dba_data_files
/
OEM
```

2. Using SQL commands within unix for loop

This construct generates backup script for a given set of datafiles in the file $OUTPUTFILE

```
for datafile in `cat $OUTPUTFILE`
do
```

```
sqlplus -s '/ as sysdba' <<EOM >>$TEMPFILE
set head off
select 'alter tablespace '||tablespace_name||' begin backup;' from dba_data_files
where file_name='$datafile'
/
!echo "beginning of racp"
select 'alter tablespace '||tablespace_name||' end backup;' from dba_data_files where
file_name='$datafile'
/
EOM
Done
```

3. while construct syntax

```
while :
do
      echo `date` >>monitor.log
      ps -ef|grep oracle|sort +3 -r >>monitor.log
      sleep 5
done
```

while :
```
  do
   read deploy_Reply?'(Y)es or (N)o? '
   case $deploy_Reply in
     Y|YES)  retval=$SUCCESS
           break ;;
     N|NO)   break ;;
     *)     ;;
   esac
  done
```

4. for loop construct

```
for i in `cat fd.lst`
do
      egrep "SPR300" $i; echo $i
done
```

5. Case construct

```
for ORACLE_SID in `cat "$DB_LIST"`
do
  case "$TARGET_NODE"
  in
```

```
prodserver ){
      CONNECT=`cat $BIN_DIR/config/connect_catp`
      };;
testserver ){
      CONNECT=`cat $BIN_DIR/config/connect_catd`
      };;
devserver  ){
      CONNECT=`cat $BIN_DIR/config/connect_catd`
      };;

   * ) echo "Not a valid Server name to run housekeeping"

 esac
echo $ORACLE_SID
export ORAENV_ASK=NO;
. /opt/oracle/product/10.2.3/bin/oraenv;
rman target / catalog ${CONNECT} <<EndRMAN>>$LogFile
      crosscheck archivelog all;
      delete noprompt expired archivelog all;
exit;
EndRMAN
done
exit;
```

22. Find documented init.ora parameters

```
set pagesize 35
set linesize 150
col NAME format a30
col VALUE format a20
col DESCRIPTION format a60
set pause on
set pause 'Hit enter to continue'

SELECT x.ksppinm NAME, y.ksppstvl VALUE, ksppdesc DESCRIPTION
FROM x$ksppi x, x$ksppcv y
WHERE x.inst_id = userenv('Instance')
AND y.inst_id = userenv('Instance')
AND x.indx = y.indx
AND SUBSTR(x.ksppinm,1,1) ^= '_'
ORDER BY 1;
```

23. Find undocumented init.ora parameters

```
set pagesize 35
set linesize 150
```

```
col NAME format a40
col VALUE format a20
col DESCRIPTION format a60
set pause on
set pause 'Hit enter to continue'

SELECT x.ksppinm NAME,
y.ksppstvl VALUE,
ksppdesc DESCRIPTION
FROM x$ksppi x, x$ksppcv y
WHERE x.inst_id = userenv('Instance')
AND y.inst_id = userenv('Instance')
AND x.indx = y.indx
AND SUBSTR(x.ksppinm,1,1) = '_'
ORDER BY 1;
```

24. List rman backups into spool file

There are few ways you could spool the rman backup into file

1. List backup from shell script

```
#!/bin/ksh
rman target / catalog rmanuser/rmanpasswd@RMANCATALOG <<EOF
>>listbkp.lst
list backup;
EOF
exit
```

2. At unix prompt

rman target / catalog rmanuser/rmanpasswd@RMANCATALOG log=listbkp.lst

RMAN>list backup;
RMAN> exit
3.Spool rman backup list to log file

rman target / catalog rmanuser/rmanpasswd@RMANCATALOG

RMAN>spool log to list_bkp.log
RMAN>list backup;
RMAN>exit